THE
CASTLE
IN THE
CLASSROOM

THE
CASTLE
IN THE
CLASSROOM

Story as a Springboard for Early Literacy

RANU BHATTACHARYYA
FOREWORD BY GEORGIA HEARD

Stenhouse Publishers
Portland, Maine

Stenhouse Publishers
www.stenhouse.com

Credits
Page xiii: "Fire," from *A Leader's Guide to Reflective Practice* by Judy
Brown, copyright © 2006 Trafford.

Library of Congress Cataloging-in-Publication Data
Bhattacharyya, Ranu, 1967–
    The castle in the classroom : story as a springboard for early literacy /
Ranu Bhattacharyya ; foreword by Georgia Heard.
        p. cm.
    Includes bibliographical references.
    ISBN 978-1-57110-770-1 (alk. paper)
    1. Language arts (Primary) 2. Reading (Primary) 3. English lan-
guage—Composition and exercises—Study and teaching (Primary) I. Title.
    LB1528.B47 2010
    372.6—dc22   2010021612

Cover, interior design, and typesetting by Martha Drury
Manufactured in the United States of America

PRINTED ON 30% PCW
RECYCLED PAPER

16 15 14 13 12 11 10   9 8 7 6 5 4 3 2 1

This book is dedicated to all my students,

Who live in places scattered all over the world

And in my heart.

You continue to inspire, awe, delight, and amaze me.

You are the original storytellers.

CONTENTS

FOREWORD

by Georgia Heard

anu Bhattacharyya begins *The Castle in the Classroom* by introducing us to the eighteen remarkable children in her kindergarten class at the American Embassy School in Delhi, India. These children come from all around the world. We meet Michelle from Taiwan, who speaks only Mandarin; Swedish Daniel, who has never been in school before; gentle Cameron from England; Roy from Israel, who is fluent in English and Hebrew, and the other fourteen children lucky enough to be in Ranu's magical classroom. As she describes each young learner, I am struck by her insights into their personalities and learning styles. Once we meet the cast of characters, like in a good play, her classroom comes alive as we turn the pages of the book; we are hooked because we care about each one of them.

As a frequent traveler to international schools, I'm always amazed by how a school can be halfway around the world from the United States, yet its children behave so similarly and have the same learning needs as American children. Although the setting and the nationalities of Ranu's students may suggest a classroom that is outside most of our experiences, these children could be kindergartners anywhere. Ranu teaches us that good teaching is good teaching, whether your students are from Taiwan or Tokyo.

Although you might never actually visit Ranu's classroom, as you read her book she paints such a distinct picture that you will feel like you're there. Here are several examples of the literacy work you will see: children enthusiastically writing stories and poems at small tables, involved in word work and other literacy center activities; children gazing into mirrors and drawing self-portraits, and then writing All About Me books; students sitting on the rug, wide-eyed and attentive, listening to *Sleeping Beauty* and *Cinderella* and other fairy tales from around the world, and later retelling and performing these fairy tales; and much, much more. You will also see that the children in Ranu's classroom are completely engaged in learning.

Fortunately, Ranu guides us in the practicalities of how to create and manage a classroom like hers. She shows us her daily schedules for reading and writing, focused literacy lesson plans, class management skills, and assessment tools. There is no doubt that she is a master of her teaching craft.

In this current climate of testing and academics, I'm struck by how Ranu's classroom is so alive; she gives her children the freedom to learn the way they do best—by playing, discovering, pretending, and exploring. Sometimes I wonder what's happened to education. Have we forgotten the fundamentals of early childhood learning, and how to create classroom environments that give young children the choice and the freedom to explore? *The Castle in the Classroom* shows us how to do this.

Here is my wish for all young children—that they can experience a class as inspiring as Ranu's. Here is my wish for all teachers—when you read *The Castle in the Classroom*, let Ranu's wise teaching be your guide.

ACKNOWLEDGMENTS

I sit to write my acknowledgments on a day when the sakura tree in our garden is in glorious full bloom. I watch the blossoms dance flirtatiously with the wind, whipping away from their moorings on the ancient gnarled tree in an attempt to rise up in the air. I watch as they hover and float, swirl and spin before gently swaying to rest on the lawn below. Much like those blossoms, when I first thought about writing this book, I had to leave my own secure moorings and take a leap into the unknown. Several people have been the "wind beneath my wings" and have given me that necessary spurt of energy to keep me afloat along the way.

For inspiring me to take that first plunge, I would like to thank Bonnie Campbell Hill. I first met Bonnie when she came to do a staff development workshop at our school. She saw some of the work we were doing in our kindergarten classroom and asked me to present my ideas at an international workshop for teachers. When I demurred, protesting I was not a public speaker, she quietly said, "Talk about what your kids are doing and the rest will follow." With her advice in mind, I presented at a few conferences, taking ideas and stories from within our classroom out to a wider audience. Buoyed by this success, I asked Bonnie what she thought I should do next. "Why, you are going to write, aren't you?" she replied in extremely matter-of-fact tones. Write? Me? I had honestly not thought about venturing into this territory at all, but Bonnie's steady belief inspired me to write up that first proposal. She has been an immense source of guidance and support since its acceptance.

I owe an incalculable debt of gratitude to Barbara Rynerson, who has been my steadfast mentor, coach, and friend. Barbara has accompanied me on my journey these past eight years, across continents, countries, and curricula, lighting my path with her extraordinary knowledge and guiding my spirit with her constant faith. Barbara opened up vistas that I had not envisioned through professional workshops and study groups, she helped me hone my vision and put it into practice, and she offered advice and commiseration when I was frustrated, helping me see my way ahead. She helped me draft that first proposal and then patiently read every version of the manuscript, providing comprehensive feedback.

For keeping me afloat through this process, I would like to thank Philippa Stratton, who has been a wonderful editor and guide. Philippa has the uncanny knack of knowing when to advise and when to applaud. She has steered this manuscript through its various incarnations and has seen it come gently to fruition. I would also like to thank Jay Kilburn and the entire team at Stenhouse for all their efforts in putting this book together. I am very grateful to Holly Holland for reading the first versions of the text. I am also very grateful to Kathy Collins, Jennifer Allen, and Lori Newman for reading subsequent versions and offering me their detailed feedback. Kathy helped me identify the heart of the book, and Jennifer helped me articulate it. Lori's clarity of thought helped clarify mine. As a fellow writer, Christina Bell offered wise and witty counsel, including timely reminders to breathe!

I have had the immense good fortune of working with fabulous teachers at many schools while the idea and then the actual writing of this book was in process. I am grateful to Sharon Taberski, who welcomed an unknown teacher from China into her classroom at the Manhattan New School and inspired her to dream. I would like to thank my colleagues at the International School of Beijing, the American Embassy School in Delhi, and the American School in Japan for their generosity, partnership, and friendship. Bob Hetzel, Susan Young, and Margaret Sood were incredibly supportive administrators at the American Embassy School who allowed me the freedom to structure and pursue my vision. I would also like to thank the students and parents of my kindergarten class at the American Embassy School for their kind permission in letting me use student photographs and artwork that add so much value to this book.

I would like to thank Georgia Heard for writing the foreword for this book. When I first heard Georgia was going to write the foreword, I was reminded of the song "I Must Have Done Something Good" from the old musical *The Sound of Music*, there being no other way to explain my feeling of inexplicable good fortune.

Finally, I would like to thank my family for their unstinting love and unwavering support. My father inspired me to aspire high and to continually strive for success, and my mother infused me with her love of words, music, and drama. My mother-in-law stood behind my dream every step of the way. My brother, Siddhartha Mukherjee, provided valuable advice at crucial moments. My son, Sujoy, an avid reader, offered insightful feedback after reading the manuscript cover to cover, and my daughter, Tinni, sustained me through long summer writing sessions, eating vanilla ice cream with chocolate sauce while watching reruns of *Grey's Anatomy*. Sanjay Bhattacharyya, my husband, greatest friend, and advocate, painstakingly read every word I wrote, and offered suggestions, recommendations—and lots of dark chocolate. The name Bhattacharyya comes from an ancient Sanskrit name that means The Keeper of the Flame. Sanjay embodies that meaning, sustaining and nurturing my flame, giving it fuel to ignite and space to shine.

In her poem "Fire," Judy Brown (2006) writes that it is fuel and the absence of fuel together that make a fire possible. A fire needs logs that are laid carefully, not packed in too tight, as well as space between those logs, "a breathing space" to make it burn:

> *A fire*
> *grows*
> *simply because the space is there,*
> *with openings*
> *in which the flame*
> *that knows just how it wants to burn*
> *can find its way.*
> (Brown 2006, 12)

Friends, thank you for helping me find the way.

PROLOGUE: STORIES HAPPEN HERE—BEWARE!

A huge castle dominates our classroom. It has tall towers and an arched doorway and seems to be built of strong stones. In the words of Roy, it has "magical powers and glows in the night." Cameron writes that "brave knights guard it" and no one can attack it. Behind the castle lies a dense forest with tall trees. Kayleigh reports that this forest is scary because the sun can't get through the trees, but it is friendly too. Many children tell each other that the forest, like the castle, also has magical powers. Far behind the forest and the castle rise mountains that are cold, with snow covering their tips. They "are slippery like glass" and are home to dinosaurs, dragons, bears, and mountain lions. At the foot of these mountains, a vast meadow meanders down to the sea. Mermaids and rainbow fish live here, and if you look close enough, you will see a golden palace. Brian, who helped construct the palace with cereal boxes and toilet-paper rolls and painted it a glittery gold, writes four pages describing its wonders.

If visitors think they have wandered into a magical fairy-tale land, they will not be far from the truth and need only look at the children's signs on our doorway. "You are entering a book," says Kimi's sign. "Stories happen here. Beware!"

Those brave enough to enter find themselves in a room that bears many hallmarks of a typical kindergarten classroom. The space is divided into two main areas—one for large-group meetings, dominated by an area rug, and another for small-group activities, set out with cozily clustered groups of tables and chairs. There is a construction and a dramatic play area, a listening center and an art center. Books abound, large and small, standing alone or in baskets. Areas and supplies are clearly labeled, in words and in pictures. There is also a small reception area, where the schedule for the day is displayed and children can sign up for the area or center in which they want to spend their time.

There are, however, some indications of a not-so-typical kindergarten classroom. The vibrant construction-paper scenes hanging from the ceiling turn the meeting area into a theatrical extravaganza. There is a play in progress there this morning. A small group of children have picked a story to perform and have selected roles and assigned a narrator. Giggling in anticipation, the audience waits for the performance to begin while there is a last-minute rush for audience seats. One child decides he would rather be a performer after all and streaks around to check the sign-up area, searching for possible openings. Discovering all the spots taken, he stoically resigns himself to watch, seating himself right at the edge of the audience, ready to sign up as soon as spots become free after the performance. As the play unfolds, it is clear that the children are adept at entering the story world and personifying it with their sensibilities. They use their own dialogue and expression as they follow the story line of a popular fairy tale. This is no rehearsed performance but an impromptu, spontaneous theater spectacle. The members of the audience, while largely respectful, throw in suggestions once in a while, some of which are seamlessly integrated into the unfolding narrative.

In the library corner, children sprawl individually and in small groups, looking at favorite books. If questioned, they will all chorus that they are reading, even though many do not have any decoding skills. The books range in genre and scope; some are clearly made by the students themselves, and these seem to be among the favorites.

At the table clusters, many activities are in progress. There is a group making masks, props, and puppets to be used in future play productions. As the children work, they make comments that indicate that they are thinking of characters in stories and what these characters should look like and what they may need. Roy has decided that he can't play his favorite mouse parts without an adequately long tail. Brian is equally absorbed in creating his swashbuckling cape. Ellali is decorating her princess tiara with plenty of glitter, sprinkling much of the sparkle generously around her.

At another table, a few children are busy writing. The table is set out with lined paper and permanent markers. There are large cards with sight words listed on them as well as picture dictionaries within easy reach. The teacher is almost invisible, supporting this group, all absolutely absorbed in writing up their own stories.

None of the groups are quiet, but none are very noisy either. The children sign up and rotate through different areas, needing minimal teacher intervention. There is a lot of movement, but children generally finish one activity before choosing another. Two underlying guidelines seem evident—don't dominate one area, and finish what you are doing before you move on.

The scene described above is midway through our kindergarten year. The children and I are immersed in our study of fairy tales. We have traveled a long way from the beginning of the year that started much the same as every other kindergarten class the world over, with a bunch of four- and five-year-olds hesitantly stepping into a new environment. Yes, we've had our share of the usual miseries and mishaps, tantrums and tears, spats and spite. But along the way we made several conscious decisions that enabled us to reach the point of independence and engagement described above. Starting a story midway through the action, however, is a guaranteed spoiler, so let's go back in time and start our story from the first day of our school year, when things were very, very different.

1

THE CAST: WHO INHABITS THIS SPACE?

Kids stream in with parents and caregivers in an ever-increasing swell. Classrooms are identified, coat hooks zeroed in on, backpacks shrugged off, and extra clothes stowed away. Shiny new lunch boxes—Barbies and Batmans emblazoned on their covers—find places in cubbies labeled with equally shiny new name tags, glued down flat and straight, no grimy curling edges yet in sight. It is the first day of school, and everything looks and feels perfect.

Yes, there are kids wailing and unwilling to separate from their parents. And, of course, many of these same parents are milling around, needing help rather than being helpful. The children, too, wander around the room exhibiting differing levels of independence and enterprise. Casting about a practiced glance, in a corner I spot two I know I will have to watch very carefully as they become best buddies and attempt to take the classroom apart. Indeed, it is overwhelmingly true that I am feeling just a little bit harried and in danger of losing my calm, professional demeanor. Why then is it so perfect? Does perfection come from seeing children move around in a space designed and created for them? Or does perfection arise from being in their company, establishing initial connections? Helping one child find his name tag, settling another with a favorite book she's recognized, starting a simple game with a group that seems fairly independent, kneeling down to greet a hesitant face peeking from behind a parent's knees.

I tell myself to be patient and wait for that magical moment when the adults will finally leave, the children will stop wailing, and we will gather together for our first meeting of the year to begin our journey toward forging a community. I know it will happen this year as it did the years before. I know I have imagined vistas of possibilities and now wait, like a dancer in the wings, to translate that vision into reality.

Let me introduce you to the children who walked into our classroom that day and whose story I tell over the next few pages. I had eighteen children in my class; most of them had just had their fifth birthday or would have it within the next two months. They were from many countries around the world. For some, this was their first move away from their home country. Others were experienced at moving—as experienced as a five-year-old can be—at settling in a new country, in a new culture, in a new school. Some had been in a playschool, a preschool, or a nursery-school program before they came to our kindergarten class; some had been homeschooled, and a few had never been in any academic setting before. Some had even been in our school's preschool program the year before. The class was divided into children whose first and only language was English, some who were fluently bilingual, and some who spoke only their native language.

Cunningham and Shagoury (2005) use the metaphor of tide pools to describe kindergartens. Just as the land and the sea meet at tide pools and organisms need to adapt to the drastic changes in environment, "children must adjust to the very different environments of home and school at this cultural meeting place. Creatures thrive in different areas of the tide pools—just as the inhabitants of a kindergarten thrive in its wide range of activities" (2005, 12). I find this metaphor uniquely applicable to my class of kindergartners every year.

Intermingling in our tide pool were children from different countries and cultures, each with distinct and unique personalities and interests. A few were hesitant explorers, investigating their new environment and trying to come to terms with it. Some were more intrepid. They had discovered their particular passions and took every opportunity to pursue their interests. Many were inquisitive inquirers, restless and curious, flitting from one activity to another, undecided and somewhat unsure. Still others were natural leaders, making decisions for themselves and their peers with enviable ease. Within the first few weeks, it became evident that the children could be sorted into broadly defined groups with some emerging common characteristics.

THE CAST OF CHARACTERS

Exploring New Environments and Discovering Self

Arnav, a bright-eyed kindergartner, had moved to Delhi over the summer from California. He had been to a preschool before, and his mother proudly said that he knew all his letters and sounds and was very excited about learning to read. Arnav loved books about animals. He was fluently bilingual in English and Hindi. He was an only child and, while very friendly and gentle, needed some support to mingle with groups.

"Franklin fell off. I did too!" confided Lizwe, showing me *Franklin Rides a Bike* by Paulette Bourgeois. That was a big speech for Lizwe, a gentle little boy from South Africa. His parents were fluently bilingual, and they told me that Lizwe understood English, as he had been to an international preschool before. His shy nature inhibited him from speaking out, but it soon became evident that Lizwe was well on his way to acquiring English not just for social usage during play, but also for articulating his comprehension and making his opinions known.

Michelle was from Taiwan. She spoke only Mandarin and, though she had been to an international preschool before, was reluctant to speak English. Her very outgoing parents could not understand what made Michelle so shy and wondered if they should employ a tutor or a speech coach. I asked for some time to help Michelle feel at home in her new environment. Michelle loved the dramatic play area and would spend most of her mornings cooking up green and yellow play-dough spaghetti. She began to speak in monosyllabic whispers, then a few words, and then complete sentences. I discovered that she could recognize the entire alphabet, upper and lower case, and could write it as well. However, she had very little experience with books and stories. Her language acquisition had been heavily academic, dependent on alphabet recognition and phonics without adequate time spent soaking in wonderful literature and glorying in songs, chants, and rhymes.

Kimi had just arrived from Denver. She had been to a preschool before and knew some letters of the alphabet. However, she was reluctant to commit to any writing even as she constructed elaborate stories with several pages of drawing stapled together. "You tell me," was her constant refrain. "I don't know how to write." In the parent survey I had asked each child's parents to fill out before the school year, Kimi's mother wrote that "Kimi loves to have playdates with her friends. She loves to pretend. She shares but has her moments of having a harder time with that."

Kayleigh and Brian were twins from Washington who had been home-schooled by their mother, a preschool teacher. Kayleigh, the more outgoing of the two, embraced her days at school with enthusiasm and energy, delighting in participating in all activities in the classroom. She almost instantly applied any new learning to her daily life, absorbing and extending it such that she took charge of her learning process independently. She recognized almost all letters of the alphabet, but not their sounds. Kayleigh had a great sense of the dramatic, and we all learned to await her pronouncements with anticipation.

Embracing Passions

Brian was the quieter twin, intensely focused, deeply motivated. Brian was a little hesitant about expressing his opinions and still more hesitant in bestowing his trust. He was very honest in his own appraisal. While he knew many letters of the alphabet and their sounds, had favorite books and loved to listen to stories, he very clearly stated that he didn't know how to read. He identified reading as figuring out the words on a page. Brian's passion was observing nature, and he spent hours at the science center, patiently and intently watching our class snails. Nobody could tell you more about those snails than Brian. His intent observation skills stood him in good stead when we started writing stories and translated into descriptions that were exact, vivid, and detailed.

Daniel was the architect of our class. He had arrived from Sweden, where he had never been to school before. Daniel built elaborate marvels with Lego blocks, intricate and space defying. He quickly became interested in learning the letters to write his name on his creations to protect them and gradually extended this interest to write up simple rules for the construction area. Daniel loved books and stories, and as I read aloud, he would seat himself as close to me as possible, staring intently at my face and the book by turns, almost in an effort to get into my skin as I read. When we later discussed the story, Daniel, with his beginning vocabulary, always had interesting observations to add.

Min Jae was from South Korea. She had been to school before and knew all her letters and sounds and had a fairly extensive vocabulary in English that she was still a little shy about trying out. Min Jae's first choice in the morning was always drawing. She would draw fabulously detailed pictures, peopled with family and friends, all happily winking away at each other in the style of Japanese anime. Min Jae was one of the first children in our classroom to make books, complete with title and end pages that she would color in all colors of the rainbow.

Jabbering furiously in Hebrew, Moria would drag her father over to our library every morning when he came to see her off. She would show him the books we had read the day before and attempt to retell the story. She seemed to soak in stories through her very being and had astonishing recall. New books would cause her to whoop with glee, and when she found ones that she had heard in her native language, her joy was a delight to behold. Moria knew no letters or sounds, but she had an amazingly rich and diverse experience in stories. She would bring in books in Hebrew to share from home and generously tell the story to any and all listeners.

Emma knew just enough letters to write her name when she joined our class. She was an endearing mixture of seriousness and fun. On one hand, she took our school and classroom values very seriously, bossing her friends in what was appropriate and what was not. On the other hand, she had a great sense of fun, delighting in song, drama, and play. Emma had a very positive attitude toward reading and writing, asserting almost from the beginning, "I am a good reader/writer." In a sense, Emma was already a member of our literacy club. She seemed to accept the wider concept of reading and writing encouraged by kindergarten teachers the world over that includes recalling and retelling favorite stories; forming opinions and connections to stories; reading signs, symbols, and labels; and creating and crafting personal stories and messages through oral language and drawing.

Driven with Curiosity

Restless and inquisitive, Ellali would flit from one activity to another every morning, losing interest almost before she began. She loved mingling with a wide group of friends and was unfailingly generous. She was fluent in Hebrew and English, often translating for friends newer to English. She had been to school before and had an incredible ear for language but mainly in its social usage. She was not interested in stories or books and even less interested in any letter acquisition. Ellali, however, loved drama and song, playacting and dressing up, and these became entry points for building her literacy skills.

Elijah loved playing in the block area, making fighter cars and "monster blaster guns." Blowing up his creations was also on his list of favorite things to do. He had been in the school's preschool program the year before, and a little bit of his reputation as a "difficult" child preceded him already. I soon discovered that Elijah could concentrate intensely when something caught his attention; unstructured times and transitions were his greatest challenges. To my great surprise and pleasure, Elijah embraced writing with fervor. Even though his motor skills were very shaky and his letter acquisition at the most basic beginner stage, Elijah's stories resounded with a voice uniquely his own. Writing seemed to calm Elijah down, giving him a purpose and focus and, ultimately, stature in the eyes of his peers. Very soon the explosions that ruled his interest and rocked our room gave way to furious scribbling.

All in the Spirit of Leadership

There are some little girls who are born to be princesses, adoring and ready to be adored, and Jasmine was one such little girl. She gave her love and trust generously, fully expecting it—and usually receiving it—back in equal measure. Jasmine embraced learning with all her being. She participated in all activities enthusiastically and then role-played my role as a teacher with her friends. Jasmine loved to read to her friends using books

I had read aloud, enthralling her audience with her sense of drama and command of the story. Jasmine was fluent in English and French. She knew some of the letters of the alphabet, especially those in her name, and some letter sounds.

Very tall, with a pure British accent and a budding sense of humor, Cameron was already a little gentleman at five. He had very strong values of what was appropriate and what was not and could lead his group toward what he perceived as fair and kind play. When he did get embroiled in rough play, he was immediately contrite and very glum. He'd tell me that he didn't think for himself! His gentle spirit and sense of justice were great leadership models for others to follow and so I encouraged him to think for himself at all times! Cameron had a very positive attitude toward books and reading, identifying himself as a "good reader" who had favorite stories. Cameron had been to a preschool in England before and had some prereading strategies. He could distinguish between words and letters and knew almost all letter names and sounds. He was aware that he could use pictures and beginning sounds to clue him into words and had also begun to build a sight-word vocabulary.

Even-tempered and friendly, Josiah was everyone's friend. He had also been in the school's preschool program along with his twin, from whom he was separated for the first time this year. It was hard to tell what Josiah loved to do most—he seemed enthusiastic and eager to try out everything. His will to learn enabled his success, and he seemed to sail through his days at school with ease. Josiah had a rich background in books and stories and knew just enough letters to write his name.

"Hey you!" was Roy's usual way to draw my attention. Wiry and energetic, Roy's tiny frame seemed to barely contain his irrepressible spirit. "You said you had eyes at the back of your head. Can't you see I am trying to say something? I also have my hand up this time!" Every time Roy wanted to say something, he could hardly wait. He had much to add to our discussions and a huge sense of fun that made classmates and adults fall in with his plans, almost willy-nilly. A born charmer, Roy was from Israel, fluent in English and Hebrew. He had been to a preschool before and knew just enough letters to write his name.

Meghan came in every morning, ready for the day, full of plans for herself and her friends. Very often she had things that she had gotten ready at home to jump-start her day—messages for her friends and teachers or little art projects to pass out. Meghan was Canadian, and her mother was a teacher. She had a rich literacy environment at home. Initially shy, Meghan blossomed into a quietly confident, articulate kindergartner. She knew all letter names and sounds and was also building up a sight-word vocabulary. She could distinguish between letters and words and predict words by using picture cues and beginning sounds. Meghan delighted in drawing and writing, and these were very often her first choices of the day.

"I no want kindergarten. I want home," was Ido's chant the first two weeks of school. He had just arrived from Israel, where he had already been in a kindergarten program for a few months, and he knew just enough English to make his disenchantment clear. Ido's parents told me that they had tried to teach him some English over the summer, but Ido—a very bright student in his native language—had been consistently resistant to the idea; to their great puzzlement, he refused to learn. His parents told me that Ido liked being in control, and I guessed that coping with a new language severely taxed his balance of power. Once Ido adapted to his classroom environment, he was able to match his peers in any activity. He combined intense energy and sheer grit in his effort to succeed.

WEAVING VARIED THREADS INTO A COMMON TAPESTRY

Our cast of characters was thus truly multinational. The members had had unique and rich life experiences, and each had his or her own distinct personality, interests, talents, and skills. Besides the themes that had already emerged within small clusters, there were others that were more universal; these were the themes that I would explore to create an ensemble that would work productively together.

In the short span of their years, many of the children had traveled across continents and cultures. These experiences were a treasure they could mine for stories. The children were such natural storytellers, retelling their experience with a sense of person, place, and time and often incorporating drama to add spice to the mixture! We heard stories about travels with brilliant sights—picking up seashells on a golden beach in Mauritius, having a snowball fight with grandparents in South Korea, rafting down a rushing river in India. These stories were grand in scale and scope, bringing the faraway, the romantic, and the fantastic into our classroom. However, these children imbued the telling of little vignettes of their everyday life with the same romance and fantasy. We heard stories of families moving and having to live out of suitcases in hotel rooms; stories of long waits for shipments to arrive; stories of families and pets left behind. Even more familiar were tales of homes, families, and siblings. Ido told us about the beautiful bathrooms in his new house where he loved taking long showers. Josiah told us how tired he was of his sister whining. Kimi mimed screaming when she saw a cockroach. Kayleigh told an enthralled class of her adventures with a wasp. Every time we heard someone's story, we added to our collective knowledge of each other. At times, one person's story served as a springboard for another. When Min Jae told us about her grandparents, many grandparent stories surfaced; similarly, Josiah's sibling woes sparked several other reminiscences.

The children, from shy Michelle to rambunctious Elijah, loved to play and could engage for hours in imaginative play of their choice. The simplest prop could serve to take the player to a different time and space zone. Wooden blocks and signs made by the children could convert a classroom rug into an elaborate city; a piece of cloth could bestow a new identity—human, animal, or alien. The children did not need fancy toys or equipment. In fact, extravagant material often hindered play, as ownership could become contentious. The children played most productively together when they had to create their own props, when they scripted their own dramatic scenarios.

The children had had varied experiences with academic literacy, in the sense of acquiring letter-sound knowledge, traditionally the thrust of early literacy. The class was divided between children who had complete knowledge of phonics but didn't really know how to apply it, children who had some knowledge of how the coding system worked, and children who had no awareness of letters and sounds at all. However, almost all the children had nonacademic traditions of literacy that they carried with them. Many of them had a rich experience with storytelling, some in their native languages, that had been part of their upbringing at home. They recognized versions of popular stories in English that they had seen in their native language. They knew songs, rhymes, and chants in languages other than English. It became clear to me that accepting and celebrating multiple tongues and traditions in our classroom would enable children who were just acquiring English to have a voice and to speak with confidence. It would unveil a treasure trove of material that would otherwise be unavailable to us. This would also balance the power equation between the English language learners and the native speakers of English, between the children who knew all of the letters and those who did not. By widening the pool of things that were unfamiliar to some and familiar to others, everyone had a chance to be an expert and everyone had a chance to be a learner.

The children's perception of what constituted a reader or a writer differed widely. Most children, with very few exceptions, did not see themselves as either. When asked to draw pictures of themselves reading at home, most children depicted cozy groups of families reading comfortably together or a child with a parent or sibling reading to them. However, reading in school was perceived as having something to do with decoding all the print correctly. Similarly, most of the children would draw joyously and spontaneously. However, when asked what they were writing, a very common response was they were not really writing because they didn't know how to spell. Real writing meant spelling out all the words correctly for others to read. For some, the task seemed so awesome that they would rather have nothing to do with it at all. A few were impatient to get on with the job and frustrated when they did not achieve immediate results. A handful had graduated to making sense of print structures and decoding successfully, and this handful could veer toward disdain for others still struggling to figure it out. It was evident that we would have to work to create a persona for a kindergarten reader and writer that went beyond traditional perceptions and accepted the differing abilities in our classroom. This persona would extend the scope of a reader to one who tells a story from a book or with a book; this persona would embrace the concept of a writer as one who creates a story orally, pictorially, or with written words.

TEACHER: CAST MEMBER OR DIRECTOR?

Who would create this persona? Who would weave the threads? As a teacher, I had the task of assigning myself a role and the choice of what that role would be. Should I cast myself as the director of this ensemble, the sole head with the complete independence as well as the responsibility of steering this performance on to success? Or should I include myself as a cast member and let the whole cast define direction? Was there a way that I could try to move between these roles? Could I be the director *and* a member of the acting cast?

Most of my childhood memories center on storytelling and imaginative play. Myths, legends, folktales, and fairy tales, heard, read, and seen, fueled fantastic worlds for my friends and me to inhabit. Stories were all around me. My grandfather would read the morning newspaper and turn current events into dramatic adventures; a favorite uncle would retell the newest thriller late into the summer night, complete with musical accents; my father would recount tales from his childhood, far from the city. Music, dance, and drama, passions inherited from my mother, provided yet more media through which I could explore stories. Learning to read opened up further vistas. Toys were limited; books were plentiful. And multiple languages were a way of life. I spoke one language at home, another with my friends, and yet another at school. Slipping between tongues, I learned to marvel at the power of language and grew to love its elasticity. As a cast member, I knew I could communicate this love to the other members.

My early childhood experiences created a lifelong love for literacy that I continued to explore in my teaching career. I immersed myself in professional research and emerged with a vision for my kindergartners that went beyond traditionally accepted definitions, one that I could translate into reality as a director of our multidimensional cast.

Traditionally kindergarten has been thought to be a place for play. There is a widely held notion that kindergarten should be *all* play and that real reading and writing starts in grade one. Another popular notion is that kindergarten is indeed a place to learn the letters of the alphabet but in an extremely limited context (such as "letter of the week"). There is also a third view, gaining currency, that of bringing down the grade one curriculum into kindergarten and doing away with imaginative play.

I argue for a slightly more novel paradigm in kindergarten education. By harnessing the natural *storytelling* enthusiasms of young children, I believe children can become readers and writers at a much younger age than originally imagined. Storytelling and story writing—both natural inclinations in children—can forge a rather effortless transition between the symbolic use of letters to their more meaningful use in real language. Indeed, the formal analogies between storytelling and sentence writing—structure, grammar, sequence, characters, space, and time—become scaffolds by which literacy is acquired more naturally rather than taught artificially. As children become storytellers, they gravitate to also becoming story writers—in effect, recapitulating. Building on children's love of story, in all its various forms (oral language, drama, reading, writing, art, interpretation, cultural traditions), can provide a strong foundation for a comprehensive literacy model in kindergarten. As Gordon Wells writes:

Stories have a role in education that goes far beyond their contribution to the acquisition of literacy. Constructing stories in the mind—or storying, *as it has been called—is one of the most fundamental means of making meaning (Bruner, 1986); as such, it is an activity that pervades all aspects of learning. When storying becomes overt and is given expression in words, the resulting stories are one of the most effective ways of making one's own interpretation of events and ideas available to others. Through the exchange of stories, therefore, teachers and students can share their understandings of a topic and bring their mental models of the world into closer alignment. In this sense, stories and storying are relevant in all areas of the curriculum.* (1985, 214)

My philosophy is grounded in the work of several teachers and authors who identified some keystones of a rich literacy program in elementary school. Several of the books that provided the foundation and inspiration for my work appear in the following box. I tried to adapt many of the ideas highlighted in these books for my kindergarten class in a way that did not just imagine the children as a slower version of a first or second grader but tapped into their intrinsic talents and interests.

Mosaic of Thought: Teaching Comprehension in a Reader's Workshop (Keene and Zimmermann 1997)
Strategies That Work (Harvey and Goudvis 2000)
Reading Essentials (Routman 2002)
Writing Essentials (Routman 2004)
The Art of Teaching Reading (Calkins 2000)
On Solid Ground (Taberski 2000)
Reading with Meaning (Miller 2002)
Units of Study for Primary Writing: A Yearlong Curriculum (Calkins et al. 2003)
Growing Readers (Collins 2004)
About the Authors (Ray 2004)
What's Next for This Beginning Writer? (Reid and Shultze 2005)

To this foundation I added the knowledge base of kindergarten teachers and authors who share my philosophy of a developmentally appropriate, literacy-rich kindergarten. In her kindergarten class, Andie Cunningham (Cunningham and Shagoury 2005) applied the model that Debbie Miller used to teach comprehension in her first-grade classroom (described in Keene and Zimmermann [1997] and Miller [2002]). Horn and Giacobbe highlight the role of "talk in and of itself" (2007, 2) as playing a powerful role in the beginning of writing.

A surprising layer added to this foundation was from outside the classroom. I have personal experience as a dancer and choreographer. As a performer on stage, I was intensely interested in the dramatization of stories through manipulating spaces and personas, juggling reality and fantasy. As a kid watcher in the classroom, I observed a similar manipulation as the children played their games of pretend, seamlessly integrating their imagined and real worlds. I wanted to harness this latent skill and put it toward developing their literacy experience.

Synthesizing research, professional experience, and personal background knowledge, my vision of literacy experience in kindergarten includes the following:

- Taking cues from the learners
- Following structures and routines to build habits
- Engaging the students in authentic reading and writing experiences
- Stressing the importance of reading and writing for a purpose
- Teaching basic skills and creating meaningful opportunities to practice those skills
- Using the spontaneous storytelling, drama, and performance instincts of children

Kindergarten literacy has been too often treated as primary school literacy. It needs to be treated separately as both play and purpose. A focus on storytelling and story writing attends to current educational demands without ignoring the developmental needs of young children.

In the following two chapters, I describe the foundations for literacy in my classroom and discuss how I launch reading and writing workshop with my kindergarten students. Chapters 4 and 5 tell the story of our immersion in fairy tales, and in Chapter 6, I review my assessment tools and we take a close look at one student, Jasmine, as she progresses through her kindergarten year, developing from an enthusiastic learner to a confident communicator.

2

SETTING
THE SCENE

E very August, I unpack my classroom supplies with a sense of anticipation and excitement. Nestled among colorful boxes of shiny new
supplies are some old samples of student work from the year past. I
have saved these to serve as exemplars for my new students, as seeing models of work actually done by their peers is one of the most effective learning
tools. Each year, I vow to browse through these later, but each year I suc-
cumb to the temptation of leafing through the carefully saved samples.

The August after I had taught the class introduced in the previous
chapter, I delve into my old samples to unearth treasure after treasure. I
find Elijah's book *Just Dad and Me*, based on a book by Mercer Mayer.

Elijah's book: "Just Dad and Me. I was playing with my dad."

"My dad won."

"I was playing soccer. I won."

Jasmine's Helen Keller book

And here is Jasmine's book about Helen Keller, based on a book by Johanna Hurwitz that Jasmine's second-grade sister read to her. Jasmine loved the story so much that she rewrote and illustrated it for her kindergarten friends. Brian thought she deserved a Caldecott medal for her work, and glued onto Jasmine's book is Brian's handmade award, carefully drawn and cut out, still glowing with glitter.

Images of the past year tumble kaleidoscopically in my mind, and I am energized for the year to come. I plan feverishly. I set up. I decorate. I anticipate. We will be the most wonderful community of readers and writers, I vow.

The samples are arranged in folders that go from the end of the year backward to the beginning. My excitement is a little tempered now as I browse the samples from early on in the year. Here the exemplars are a little rougher around the edges. I find signs that the children had made for areas around the room and rules to make these areas function. I chuckle as I read Josiah's advice to his classmates that was pasted over the fish tank all year.

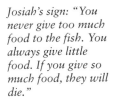

Josiah's sign: "You never give too much food to the fish. You always give little food. If you give so much food, they will die."

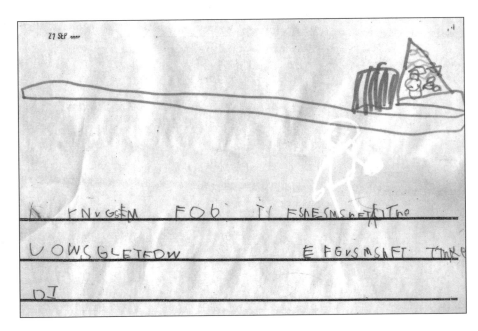

Delving further into the box, I reveal letters that the children had written to each other or to me. I sigh as I unfold Cameron's note.

Cameron's letter: "Dear Mrs. Ranu, I love your clothes and you are the best teacher. Love from, Cameron."

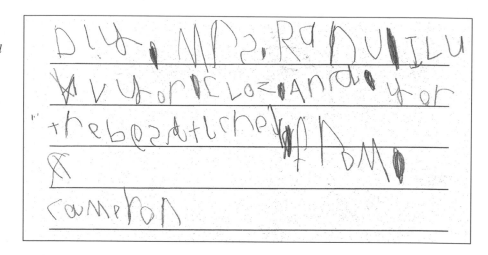

Expressing admiration for my clothes and commenting on my teaching? That boy sure knew the way to my heart, didn't he? Burrowing deeper, I discover the children's first attempts at stories.

This act of unpacking has come to be a very deliberate and symbolic act for me. I cherish the vision of possibilities it unfolds—possibilities yet to be discovered in the year to come. At the same time, it cautions me not to be caught up in the glorious images of May as I begin with a new group of students in September.

As I plan for the year, I divide routines, structures, and materials into those that I will set up by myself and those that I will set up with my students in the first four to six weeks of the year.

BY TEACHER	WITH STUDENTS
Divide classroom into separate learning environments (e.g., library, writing area, dramatic play area) with some materials denoting each area.	Unpack materials for the learning areas.

Assign a sign-up system for using the areas and the number of children that each space can accommodate. Establish routines for the sign-up system.	Decide on rules for using each space and consequences for violating those rules. Write and publish rules for each area.
Set aside a time to establish community guidelines over the first four to six weeks.	Develop community guidelines.
Plan a balanced schedule for each day.	Check the schedule to recognize patterns and learn to anticipate events.
Plan times to meet and confer with each student over the course of a week or as needed.	Establish signals that indicate that conference times are sacred times between individual students and teacher. Others must engage themselves during this time. Model problem-solving strategies should problems occur during this time.

A BALANCED LITERACY MODEL

The instructional model that I follow is the balanced literacy model. In her book *One Child at a Time,* Pat Johnson (2006) says that a balanced literacy approach does not mean an eclectic program with pieces from every other method of teaching. With reference to reading, for instance, *balance* refers to having a balance in your program of *whose responsibility it is to do the reading work.* In other words, how much responsibility for figuring out the words and comprehending the meaning is the job of the teacher and how much is the job of the students?

The balanced literacy model enables a gradual release of responsibility from teacher to student through the contexts of shared reading, interactive reading, guided reading, and independent reading; shared writing, interactive writing, guided writing, and independent writing. The model emphasizes explicit teaching of strategies through focus lessons, followed by students engaged in guided and independent practice. The teaching context is a balance between whole-group, small-group, and independent activities. I adopted this model for our classroom but reworked its components to best suit the needs of my very young learners.

Reading

Shared reading is a whole-group activity. Besides reading Big Books, we also use songs placed on hanging easels and play games on the white-board or magnetic board. The children participate in reading the text and problem-solve letters, sounds, and words in a shared context. Interactive

read-alouds maintain the whole-group context but add partner work while making meaning. During interactive read-aloud, I read a book aloud and think aloud about my developing understanding and at intervals invite the children to contribute their thinking. At times, I ask them to work with their partners "eye to eye, knee to knee" to build their thinking together. A precocious member of our class figured out that the initials of this activity spelled *EEKK*, and since that day all I have to do is murmur, "I wonder what is happening. . . . Eekk!" as a signal for my kindergartners to turn and talk. During interactive read-aloud, we work mainly on comprehension skills.

Guided reading shifts the context to small-group work. I pull groups together that have similar needs, and these groups change through the year. Independent reading is an opportunity

for the students to practice the skills they are acquiring through the above contexts in an independent way. The children have access to reading material throughout the classroom: books we have read together or that are placed in baskets labeled by genre, theme, or author; leveled baskets of "just-right" books; books we have made together as a class; books the children have made individually; and songs and charts hanging up in the room. During independent reading, I move around the room and confer with the children as needed.

Writing

The writing contexts mirror the reading contexts, and the focus progresses from whole-group to small-group to independent work. During shared writing, the students and I create text as a group. I actively model writing, thinking aloud about my strategies, problems, and choices. I invite students' suggestions and incorporate these in my writing. During interactive writing, the children and I take turns holding the pen and create text together. A whole-group activity, interactive writing is an opportunity for the children to "give it a go" in a supported, safe environment.

I mostly conduct guided writing lessons through table conferences while the children are writing independently at their tables. These table assignments are the same as their regular seating assignments. They are social in nature and change regularly so that the children get the opportunity to work and collaborate within different groupings. During a table conference, I identify a broad skill needed by the entire group, such as leaving finger spaces between words. I coach the children on this particular skill and then invite them to try it out before I move on to the next group. Table conferences enable me to touch base with a large portion of my class and pave the way for successful, uninterrupted individual conferences.

MAPPING IT OUT

I fit all the components into a yearlong road map. The Kindergarten Literacy Overview form (Figure 2.1; see Appendix) takes the kindergarten year and divides it into three trimesters and three contexts: the reading workshop, the writing workshop, and word-study centers. The first trimester focuses on establishing the reading and writing workshops, emphasizing routines and attitudes that I hope to follow all year-round. I start the year by focusing on stories from our lives and read stories that relate to our lives as well. We practice storytelling with stories we know best, those from our lives and those about things we love. During the second trimester, we start reading fairy tales as a natural extension of storytelling. We add drama and performance as an added dimension, and later we incorporate all these elements to write our own fairy tales. In the third trimester, the focus shifts to extending our reading and writing personas.

There is a natural progression of skills and strategies taught, keeping in mind the developmental needs of the children and their expanding level of expertise through the year. Reading and writing and word study are intimately connected. I have defined separate essential questions for each context in each trimester. Since I know what my big focus is for each trimester, I don't scramble around for books to suit focus lessons but can choose to apply the focus lessons to books we have in our classroom library. My preparation is very simple as the books, materials, and games are in the classroom all year-round.

I remember my earliest teaching days when I would consult various manuals about themed activities or literacy centers that integrated art, reading, and writing. Stenciling shapes, cutting them out, setting up centers, handing out material, explaining sets of instructions, and clearing up left me exhausted at the end of the day. I was also aware of a niggling sense that my kids were not really getting it even though the manuals promised lofty returns in terms of reading and writing achievement.

FIGURE 2.1: KINDERGARTEN LITERACY OVERVIEW

	Reading Workshop	Writing Workshop	Word-Study Activity Centers
TRIMESTER 1	*Exploring the workshop: What are books? What are readers? Who reads? Where do we read? What do we read? How do readers get the message?* *Shared-reading focus* • Making book choices • Introducing reading strategies *Read-aloud focus* • Personal narratives • Realistic fiction *Comprehension focus* • making text-self connections *Student focus* • Reading behaviors • Book knowledge • Independent reading/partner reading	*Exploring the workshop: What is writing? Where do we find writing? Who writes? Why do writers write? How do we write?* *Focus lessons* • Writing process *Genre focus* • Personal narratives and recounts *Celebration* • Author party within class • Individual personal narratives published	*Introducing early literacy concepts, letters, and sounds* • Recognizing and learning names • Hearing words in a sentence • Exploring, recognizing and naming, learning and making letters • Hearing rhymes • Hearing syllables • Stretching words to hear sounds • Hearing beginning sounds
TRIMESTER 2	*Expanding the workshop: How do stories work?* *Shared-reading focus* • Consolidating reading strategies • Expanding reading strategies *Read-aloud focus* • Fairy tales and fiction *Comprehension focus* • Making text-to-text connections *Student focus* • Home reading	*Expanding the workshop: How do writers write stories?* *Focus lessons* • Story planning • Story writing • Story language *Genre focus* • Fairy tales and pretend stories *Celebration* • Author party with parents and wider community • Storybook published	*Manipulating letters and sounds* • Hearing ending sounds • Making rhymes • Hearing middle sounds • Two-letter word families • Recognizing, building, and writing high-frequency words
TRIMESTER 3	*Extending the workshop: How do readers pursue their interests?* *Shared-reading focus* • Using reading strategies • Strategies leading toward deeper understanding *Read-aloud focus* • Favorite author studies • Genre studies (nonfiction, poetry) *Comprehension focus* • Making text-to-life connections *Student focus* • Guided reading • Book clubs	*Extending the workshop: How do writers express themselves through different genres?* *Focus lessons* • Writer as teacher • Shaping writing to fit genres • Expressive word choices *Genre focus* • Writing nonfiction and poetry *Celebration* • Author party with older and younger buddies • Individual "how-to" books, "all about" books; class poem book published	*Integrating and consolidating letter, sound, and word knowledge* • Making and breaking sentences • Onsets and rimes • Upper case/lower case letters • Alphabetical order • Three-letter word families • Color, number, week words • Word structures—plurals • Word solving and making connections

Where was I going wrong? My mistake, I now know, was fragmenting the time into discrete elements. One activity or project flowed into another, but the children were not being given enough time to master one set of skills before we embarked on the next. I was so anxious to keep my instruction varied and creative that I forgot that repeated practice embeds skills and scaffolds further learning.

Using the Kindergarten Literacy Overview as my road map for the year helps me see how the exploration of a set of skills lends itself to the expansion of those skills and then ultimately to their extension into other areas. The children's level of expertise grows as there are plenty of opportunities for practice and choice in familiar settings. Yet there is variety in the structure through the focus lessons where different skills are taught, varied strategies practiced, and multiple genres encountered. The children are intimately familiar with all the material—books, classroom supplies, games, math manipulatives, and construction and dramatic play props—because we have unpacked it together and established rules of usage. This results in shared understanding of how our space operates and leads to a shared investment in maintaining it.

LAYING THE FOUNDATION: BUILDING THE READING AND WRITING HABIT

Emma walks into the classroom, clutching a little sticky note tightly in her hand. She has a worried frown but a determined air. Slipping her name card into a free slot for the writing center, she heads straight for the materials, picks out some plain white paper and some markers. She carefully smooths out her crushed sticky note and then starts writing vigorously. I peek over her shoulder to ask her what she is composing. "Well, my uncle's dog died and he is very sad. I am writing him a letter with a dog picture so he will feel better." Gesturing to the note, Emma adds, "Look, I asked my mom to write my uncle's name and the dog's. I think he should get another dog and call it the same." Emma painstakingly sounds out each word in her letter, using mostly beginning sounds, checking out the alphabet chart several times to form her letters. She copies the names from her sticky note. As she nears the end, she pauses for a second, and then I see her jump up and rush to the word wall to locate and copy the word *and*. Emma finishes her note with a flourish and asks me to remind her to take it home to give to her mom to post. Out of the corner of my eye I notice several children have been watching our interaction thoughtfully, and I sense that we are in for a letter-writing flurry in our classroom. I am not mistaken; the very next day, Kimi and Meghan walk in clutching sticky notes!

♜ ♜ ♜

I have a vision for the children in my care. I imagine every child in our classroom will think of himself or herself as a reader and writer and participate, perform, grow, and celebrate in a literate world, surrounded and supported by a community of learners. In its simplest interpretation, this vision celebrates a reader as a person who interacts with print on his or her own terms—choosing books and making meaning. As a writer, he or she creates meaning and communicates thinking through print and pictures.

Emma personifies that vision in many ways. Reading and writing are a means for her to connect to the larger world. She knows that she can use writing to create meaning that others can then read. She also knows that certain words can be read only if written correctly and devises a way to help her do so. Despite having only the most basic literacy skills, Emma is not at all hesitant about plunging in at the deep end. Celebrating her adventures in her ever-expanding literary pool inspires her classmates to do the same.

SCHEDULING READING AND WRITING WORKSHOPS

I schedule reading and writing workshops from the very first day of the school year. However, I rework the basic workshop model for elementary classes to suit the needs of my learners. A typical full day (8:30–3:00) in our kindergarten would have the following components:

Free Choice (45 minutes)
Reading Workshop (60 minutes)
Literacy Stations (45 minutes)
Writing Workshop (60 minutes)
Math Centers/Science Centers (60 minutes)
Specials and Breaks—PE, Music, Art, Lunch, etc. (30 minutes)

BUILDING THE READING HABIT

The first part of the reading workshop is shared reading (fifteen minutes), in which we look closely at letters, sounds, symbols, words, and rhymes.

FIGURE 2.2: SHARED-READING WEEKLY PLAN

	Monday	Tuesday	Wednesday	Thursday	Friday
Sing	Old song on teaching easel Work on quick-and-easy words	*New song on teaching easel*	Tuesday's song on easel Work on quick-and-easy words	*New song on hanging easel*	Thursday's song on hanging easel Work on sentences/ words/letters
Read	*Alphabet Story* Shared writing	Old Big Book Old reading strategy	*New Big Book* Introduce new reading strategy	Wednesday's book Reinforce new reading strategy	Old alphabet story
Play	Old game from reading station	Old game from reading station	Old game from reading station	Old game from reading station	*New game*

Words in italics are the new things taught.

During this time we build up our word study skills. In these fifteen minutes, we read a Big Book, sing a song, and play a literacy game as a group. The books I choose to read and the songs we sing target community goals. The games we play build literacy skills as well as help model taking turns, listening to others, and demonstrating expertise in front of an audience. These games become part of our literacy stations, and the children practice playing them in small groups or independently. (See Figure 2.2.)

I follow up shared reading with literacy stations (forty-five minutes). The children rotate through these stations and practice alphabet and word skills through a series of games, using a variety of manipulatives. Most of the games and manipulatives are kept on the shelves all year long, and the children can access them during free choice as well. The children are able to engage at literacy stations independently, as we have established sign-ups and routines for rotations. We have the simplest sign-up system with different areas defined by a picture of the activities and/or the materials to be found there. Among the areas offered are choices popular in most kindergarten rooms such as the block area; the dramatic play corner; the math center; the painting, art, and craft center; and the science center. However, there are also many choices that focus on literacy skills, such as reading Big Books, practicing rhymes and songs, playing word games, using the listening center, storytelling with props, and working in the writing center. The library is always open as a choice as well. I laminate the sign-up cards, cut slots with a paper cutter, and slide in jumbo metal paper clips into the slots to assign the number of players each area can hold. Most areas are limited to four to six children at a time. All the students have individual name cards that they can slide onto a paper clip as long as one is available. They can rotate according to their choice, but I hold each child responsible for moving only their own name card, never that of a classmate, no matter how great the temptation may be to nudge somebody out and slide themselves in! Barring a few dramatic denouements, the children generally rise to this responsibility and love exercising their choice.

We all know the huge role choice plays in achievement, and while the children gravitate naturally to areas they are most interested in, they become open to experiencing others. Seeing their own and their classmates' name cards on a daily basis is also a great way to learn to recognize all those names. Playing alongside a favored friend becomes another factor in exercising choice. The ensuing response and dialogue between the children plays a decisive role in their learning and creates the necessary energy to sustain our learners in the challenges they face. As the children are productively engaged in play of their own choosing, alongside peers whose company they have sought, monitored by classmates who have shared understandings, I am able to work with small groups of children and confer and coach as needed.

Shared reading and the literacy stations build strategies to decode print. At the same time, reading behaviors and comprehension strategies are targeted through interactive read-alouds (fifteen minutes) and independent reading (twenty minutes) that also form an essential part of the reading workshop. The time spent reading independently increases as the year progresses. I also build in a share time (ten minutes), when the children share their thoughts, discoveries, opinions, and connections about the books they've been browsing through. This is an especially valuable time because it builds our collective knowledge of books and of ourselves as readers.

FOCUS LESSONS

The separate contexts of the reading workshop—shared reading, literacy stations, interactive read-aloud, and independent reading—have separate though interconnected, interdependent focus lessons. The focus lesson strategies taught by the teacher through shared reading and interactive read-alouds are practiced by the students through literacy stations and independent reading. The focus lessons from the beginning of the year set

Reading Strategies anchor charts listing and explaining the lessons hang around the room as reference points for the students to use throughout the year.

up the reading workshop in slow stages. The goal is to build a reading habit and identify some strategies to enable the children to do so. I have designed these focus lessons to perform several tasks simultaneously in those crucial first few weeks of the school year. The lessons not only target literacy goals but also build community in the classroom and establish ownership of the space.

As a reader, I think *within* the text. I solve words, monitor and correct, search and use information, and summarize. I also think *beyond* the text. I make connections to characters and events, predict, infer, and synthesize. Moreover I think about the text. I analyze the author's style and craft and critique the ideas incorporated in it (Fountas and Pinnell 2006). These are the reading habits that I need to model for my students. I try to do so in a systematic, phased manner that builds in complexity as the year unfolds.

Among the reading habits that I want the students to build early on in the year is the ability to negotiate books on their own terms. I want them to approach text with confidence, certain that they will be able to make meaning. I want the children to be able to think about books and to share their thinking. I also want them to exercise choice in a conscious manner. Besides these habits, I want the children to build strategies to read.

FOCUS LESSON | *Readers Form Opinions and Talk About Books*

Purpose | *To learn to form and express opinions about books and stories*

Lesson | *Model a book talk about a favorite book.*

Student Extension | *Students bring in favorite books to class to share.*

I start off the kindergarten year reading the Rainbow Fish series of books by Marcus Pfister. I love these stories for their message of how an individual can become a part of a community. I also read the Franklin books by Paulette Bourgeois. Franklin the turtle encounters problems and faces issues familiar to many of my young students. My other favorites are the Little Critter series by Mercer Mayer and all the books by Kevin Henkes. As I read these books to the children, I model my thinking aloud and invite comments and opinions from them.

During the first week, I ask the children to bring in their favorite stories from home to share. We sit in a circle, facing each other, with our books in front of us. I tell the children that as I read, I constantly think about whether I like the book or not. I deliberately do not go into details at this stage but keep it very simple. I model how to book-talk my book. I hold aloft *The Rainbow Fish* by Marcus Pfister and describe how this is one of my favorite books. The story is about the rainbow fish, the most beautiful fish in the ocean, with the loveliest glittering, sparkling scales. But the rainbow fish is very proud of his scales and doesn't like to share them with the other fish. After a while the other fish start ignoring him, and the rainbow fish becomes the loneliest fish in the ocean. The wise old octopus who lives in a dark cave advises him to begin sharing his scales, and so he does. He loses the things he was most proud of but finds friends instead. I tell the children that I really like the way the rainbow fish changes his behavior and finds friends toward the end of the story. I share my favorite illustration from the book.

I then invite the children to share their books, following my example: hold the book aloft, share a little bit about the story and perhaps a favorite picture. We go around the circle. Meghan has brought in her Disney princess stories. "I really like chapter books about princesses," she confides. Jasmine excitedly shares that she too loves reading about princesses and fairies, though the book she has chosen to bring in is about animals. Arnav talks about Thomas, the tank engine; and Brian has a book about bird watching. He tells us he has been trying to find all the birds that are in it!

As we go round the circle, I start getting a sense of the reading interests of my students. We begin to identify books by broad themes—princesses, trains, animals, teddy bears, families, and so on—and the children begin to understand that there are others in our classroom who have interests similar to their own. They begin to get excited about some choices that are unfamiliar to them as they hear the other children speak about their books. ♜

FOCUS LESSON | *Readers Make Connections as They Read*

Purpose   *To decide whether the book they are reading reminds them of something that happened in their own life, in another book, or in the world around them and to realize that sometimes these connections spiral and build on one another*

Lesson   *Model own connections to books while reading aloud.*

Student Extension   *Children share their own connections to books.*

I continue reading the Rainbow Fish books as we work on our community guidelines. The focus, as in any other kindergarten classroom, is to play and work productively in a group, cooperating and problem solving as necessary. To make a group work, we need to learn how to get along. To learn how to get along, we need to become aware of what other people are thinking and feeling and communicate our thoughts and feelings to them. Since our faces provide clues to our feelings, I try to make the children as aware as possible of messages that we may receive from other people's faces. We playact and look at pictures to understand how emotions can be "read" by certain clues. While reading stories, I ask the children to focus on the pictures of particular characters and try to guess what they may be feeling and whether these pictures remind them of a time they've felt the same way. This feeds right into reading comprehension, as the children make text-to-self connections that help them understand the story better. It also aids our community-building effort. The children learn to recognize, accept, and cope with the feelings characters in books and in real life encounter and learn that the same situation can give rise to different feelings in different people.

The children become increasingly confident about sharing their connections, and those connections make stories a part of our lives. Kayleigh looks at *Franklin in the Dark* and guesses that sometimes you may be "grumpy and sad and worried at the same time," and that's when you have a "frowny" face. Brian, while reading a story about a baseball game, predicts that the character was feeling happy as he "was high-fiving his friend." Elijah, while reading *No, David!* by David Shannon, says that he knew how the mom was feeling when David bothered her because his mom felt mad when his brother bugged her too. He said this with such an angelic expression that I didn't dare ask how she felt when he bothered her! Roy shares that the little critter in *Just Me and My Dad* by Mercer Mayer was scared as he was looking over his shoulder, and then he acts it out for us. Emma talks about how *Julius, the Baby of the World* by Kevin Henkes reminds her of the time that her baby sister was born and she was really jealous. She predicts that now that they are about to have another baby in the family, her little sister will probably feel the same way.

"Franklin wants a pet. It reminds me of when I wanted my dog."

I model text-to-text connections by reading books with similar themes. I then invite children to share their own connections between books. Kimi shares how *No Matter What* by Debi Gliori and *Mama, Do You Love Me?* by Barbara Joosse are similar because the characters in both ask their moms whether they would love them if they turned into polar bears! Emma proudly comes up to tell me, "I am going to make a really good connection. In *Franklin Goes to School* and *Countdown to Kindergarten*, they are both scared to go to school because they can't tie their shoes." Meghan has another Franklin book, *Franklin Is Bossy*, and she says that it reminds her of another book we've been reading, *The Land of Many Colors* by Rita Pocock, as the characters in both are mean to each other and bossy. I can never forget Arnav's text-to-self connection to *The Land of Many Colors*. The story is about different-colored people—the blue, the purple, and the green—who like things only in their particular color. They live segregated lives and can't get along and finally end up going to war. This results in much trouble and many shortages, especially of food. A little boy whose body is so covered with the dust of war that his color is indeterminate tries to stop the destruction. "Why are we fighting?" he asks. "We are all the same." The different-colored people find that ending the war and pooling their resources brings an end to their problems. Arnav, while poring over the pictures of the book, realized that the first few illustrations of the people did not show their hearts, while the illustrations toward the end had all the hearts painted in. Arnav gravely told me, "They opened their hearts. We should do that too." "Open your hearts" became our classroom mantra from then on and one of our community rules! ♜

FOCUS LESSON

Readers Choose Books Carefully

Purpose　To make conscious and informed choices about reading and use various strategies to choose books

Lesson　Model the strategies in the following table.

STRATEGIES	MODELING
Look at the cover.	I concentrate on the cover of a book. I describe the pictures I see on it and predict that the book will probably be about some of these pictures.

Look at the title.	I gather together books that are in the same series or about the same character. I look at the titles and demonstrate how I can "read" the title by putting together the name of the character and the picture on the cover.
Look at the pictures.	I read a picture book by only looking at the pictures and following the story through the pictures.
Look at the words.	I pick out a book that has many easy sight words and exclaim that this is a book that I can read all by myself.
Choose a book you've heard before.	I place all the books I've read aloud on a shelf next to my teaching easel and demonstrate how that is an easy access point to find familiar books. I extend the discussion and tell the students that they can also choose books they've heard from their family members and friends.

Student Extension

Classroom book sort and organization of the classroom library

I want the children to use the library productively and independently. We begin the year with a limited number of books out on the library shelves and in the book baskets. Over the initial few weeks, we spend a lot of time talking about books and how we can identify them by subject, theme, or author. I have some books sorted out in baskets, but I save the majority for sorting as a class. I spend a week modeling choosing books and putting them back in the correct basket. The baskets have colorful labels and illustrations to identify them. Some are categorized and labeled by a broad theme: family stories, school stories, animal stories, friendship stories, earth stories, alphabet stories. Some are author based: Eric Carle, Leo Lionni, Kevin Henkes, Mercer Mayer. Still others are character based: Franklin stories, Rainbow Fish stories, Clifford stories. Some are by genre: information books, fairy tales, poetry.

I tell the children that as readers we know that we all have favorite books and things we like to read about. The classroom library is organized so that we can quickly choose books, so we need to put them back correctly to make sure everybody can find them easily. I tell the students that we are all going to be responsible for our classroom library. Over the course of the following week, I go through different strategies to model choosing books: look at the cover; look at the title; look at the pictures; look at the words; choose a book you've heard before. I put up these strategies on anchor charts around our room, and after these lessons, we begin sorting boxes of books for the classroom library. We practice all that we have learned. The children become very familiar with the books as they go through them and decide where to place them. There are spirited discussions and arguments. As much as possible, I let the children make the decisions and mold the library into their own space. ♜

FOCUS LESSON | Readers Value Books and Their Reading Time

Purpose   *To establish independent reading habits*

Lesson   *Model the strategies in the following table.*

STRATEGIES	MODELING
Start from the first page.	I demonstrate how I miss huge chunks of the story if I start the book anywhere I please. I emphasize that I turn pages in sequence, starting from the first page.
Turn pages one by one.	I deliberately skip pages and read a story that is missing logical transitions. I then demonstrate that I need to turn pages one by one.
Put books back where you find them.	I show a labeled basket of books that has books placed in there by

mistake and ask the children whether it would be easy to find the books we need if all the baskets in our library got so mixed up. I stress that we need to put books back where we find them to make it easier for everyone to use the shared library.

Use library voices.

We establish shared understandings of "inside" voices—those that we can use to play and work inside; "outside" voices—those that we can use on the playground; and "library" voices—those that we use during reading workshop. We debrief after reading workshop to discuss how successful our use of library voices has been.

Read with one partner.

I role-play successful versus unsuccessful partner reading with a volunteer. The students and I brainstorm how to choose books together; how to share and hold books by sitting next to each other appropriately; how to turn pages together; how to put books back together.

Student Extension

Students practice reading independently.

A hush falls over the room as independent reading time commences. I have been modeling how readers value their reading time, and we have proceeded through a series of strategies: start from the first page, turn pages one by one, put books back where you find them, use library voices, and read with one partner. Children are sprawled around the room in various positions. Some have created cozy nooks for themselves with cushions, and a few sit at tables; still others giggle mysteriously with a partner. Each child has a pile of books nearby that he or she browses through with different levels of engagement and expertise.

My eye follows Ellali, who wanders about the room. She picks up a book from the library, flicks through the pages desultorily before dropping it back down. She tries to nudge her friend near her, who is curled up around a cushion. Receiving no reaction, she sighs dramatically and goes back to the library and looks without favor at all the books arrayed for her choice.

I walk up to Ellali and whisper, "Have you found something you like?" Ellali is thrilled to have someone finally notice her plight. "I can't find anything. I can't read!" she wails. I ask Ellali whether she would like to read with me. She chooses *The Yellow Balloon* by Charlotte Dematons, a marvelously illustrated wordless picture book. We curl up on the carpet with Ellali holding the book aloft. I let her turn the pages and ask her to tell me what she notices about the pictures. Slowly, Ellali begins to string the pictures together and, by the third page, figures out a narrative structure. "This story is about the balloon going around the world!" she exclaims. Her feeling of empowerment is contagious, and there is a momentous thrill of connection between two readers—teacher and student—who understand the same message by an author. "How did you figure that out?" I ask her. She replies promptly, "I looked at the pictures." I congratulate Ellali on reading the book by herself, and she proudly decides to share her discovery with her friends at the end of independent reading time. Though I realize that I will still have to continue monitoring Ellali, I know that in the future, she will be able to use her time better because she has discovered there is a way for her to successfully engage with a book independently. She now has at least one concrete strategy that she can further practice and refine. Sharing her success with her friends makes this path accessible for many of my other students, who may perhaps be facing the same issue. ♜

BUILDING STRATEGIES TO READ

Curling up with a book and pretending to read can sustain independent reading for only a short while, and my students need to actively have some strategies to decode text to continue to be successful. Through shared reading of Big Books and songs, we proceed through a series of focus lessons to explicitly break down strategies to read. Some of the lessons that work well in our classroom are outlined in the following table.

STRATEGIES	MODELING
Look at the pictures.	I cover up words in a Big Book, and the children and I read the story by looking at the pictures. We read the words later to confirm our initial reading.
Look at the words.	I cover up some key words that match pictures in a Big Book and deliberately misread them. The children protest loudly since it is obvious that I am reading incorrectly. I sigh dramatically and fix my gaze on the line of text. I uncover the text as I read, reading the correct words this time.
Stretch words like a rubber band and sound them out. • Look at the word and the pictures. • Look at the beginning part of a new word, and check it with the pictures. • Go across the word from beginning to middle to end. • Look for chunks in words. • Reread.	I cover some words in a Big Book, leaving their initial letter but changing the rest of the word (like changing *cow* into *cat* and *duck* into *dog* in *Mrs. Wishy-Washy* by Joy Cowley). I read the text incorrectly. "Look at the pictures! They don't match," clamor the children. I do an obvious double take and start afresh, modeling how I match the words with the pictures. I model how I focus on the beginning sound and get my mouth ready to say it. I use a rubber band to show how I stretch out the words from beginning to middle to end and offer rubber bands to the children to help them do the same. I usually follow up this lesson with a similar one on word endings.
Read "quick-and-easy words."	"Quick-and-easy words" is our class term for words we encounter all the time in our reading and writing. They are usually

continued

known as sight words. I teach recognition of these words through our daily song routines. After we become familiar with a song, I cover up some of the sight words and invite children to fill them in as we sing. Since rainbow fish is a theme we follow in our classroom, I paste the sight words as scales on rainbow-fish-shaped cards and laminate them. We focus on one word at a time as we go through the list, but they are all available for use at all times at our literacy stations, on the word wall, and on anchor charts.

Read words you recognize.

We start the year focusing on the names of the students in our class. Through daily song and game routines, these become a bank of words that the children recognize instantly. The children also have many opportunities to "read around the room," using fancy pointers, giant spectacles, and binoculars. Some children come with a bank of words they already know, but for others this is their first exposure to letters and words.

BOOK BAGS

Two more things aid independent reading time in our classroom. One is book bags. Each child has a clear plastic folder—or book bag—that I cover at the beginning of the year and label with the child's name. I then encourage the children to personalize their folders so that they are instantly recognizable. These contain a selection of books that are "just right" for students to practice reading with and also include books they've heard me read aloud that may be higher than their actual reading level but that they can retell since they are familiar with the story. The book bags can also contain books that enable children to practice storytelling by just looking at the pictures.

When independent reading time starts, the children pick up their book bags and settle down with their selection. I ask them to practice with their just-right books first and then spend some time browsing through their other choices. We switch over to partner reading after ten minutes of independent reading time; children have the option to continue reading independently in their chosen spot or read with a partner for ten minutes. During these twenty minutes, I confer with individual students and practice reading with them one on one. I check through their book-bag selections and make recommendations. Usually a reading conference is followed by a shopping trip to the classroom library, where the children restock their book bags following the suggestions mentioned during the conference.

READING FOLDERS

The children carry home the books that they have practiced reading with me in their reading folders. The reading folder is a simple two-pocket folder that includes a dated reading log that I fill out for the child and that the parents sign at home. Within the folder, I include a list of strategies that the parents can use at home as their child reads to them. These strategies mirror the ones we use in the classroom as well. They include the following suggestions:

- Allow your child to "tell the story" not always reading the words, as this is an early stage of reading.
- Discuss the story, characters, and the best parts.
- Encourage your child to find specific letters on a page.
- Count the number of words on a page.
- Encourage your child to find a word on a page by looking for the beginning letters.
- Ask your child whether the story reminded them of something that happened in their lives or in another book.

The student and I decide on a bookmark to place with the book before it goes home. There are three choices of bookmarks available in our class. They are in three different colors and state very simply, "I can read this book all by myself," or, "I need some help reading this book," or "Please read this book to me." Home reading is an extension and celebration of the reading personas the children have been developing at school. It is not meant to be homework; rather, it is meant to ignite and keep aglow the flame of reading that Mem Fox refers to when she says, "The fire of literacy is created by the emotional sparks between a child, a book, and the person reading" (2008, 10).

3

WRITING
THE SCRIPT

The writing focus lessons at the beginning of the year essentially mirror the reading focus lessons; I want the students to see themselves as both readers and writers. Similar to readers who read for different purposes, writers write for different purposes, and they use many strategies to communicate their message: they write by drawing pictures, by sounding words out, by referencing quick-and-easy words, and by writing words they recognize. They try writing the best they can. Readers use similar strategies to read: they use pictures, sound words out, learn to recognize quick-and-easy words, and read the best they can. Writers share their stories with a larger community through publishing; readers share their ideas about books through summarizing and synthesizing. The strategies modeled through the focus lessons hang as anchor charts around our room. I deliberately use the same icons to illustrate both the reading strategies and the writing strategies, and each year this deliberation is rewarded when some students make the connection and exclaim, "But they are the same!" This discovery paves the way for a discussion on how the skills to build reading and writing have similar sources.

The first set of focus lessons for writing builds the writing habit and gives the students some strategies to use. Over the course of the first two weeks, I offer the children several opportunities to write about concrete experiences. The focus is on thinking of an idea and reproducing it faithfully on paper.

Our writing workshop is about sixty minutes long. I start by gathering the children for a fifteen-minute focus lesson where I model a particular strategy. This is followed by independent writing, during which time the children move to their assigned table spots and write independently while I move around and confer in table groups or individually. I gradually increase this time from a tight fifteen minutes ("Oh my goodness! Can you believe our writing time is over!") the first few weeks to a lengthier thirty minutes once the children have a few writing strategies under their belt. We then gather for fifteen minutes while the children share their writing with their classmates.

Setting up the workshop, establishing the pattern of focus lessons followed by independent practice, modeling strategies to draw and write, demonstrating proper use of materials, and expanding possibilities to be productively and independently engaged when students are done with their writing takes about two to three weeks. In the meantime, we are steeping ourselves in stories during reading workshop. We identify themes in stories and make connections between the stories and our own lives. As the children share their connections, I always wonder out loud whether that is something they may like to write about later. Slowly we come to an understanding that we all are treasure troves of stories waiting to be shared, and then we are ready for our foray into writing personal narratives.

BUILDING THE WRITING HABIT

I start off the kindergarten writing year with a focus on talking about my ideas out loud and drawing. As with the reading workshop, we begin from the very first day of school. The children have writing folders where they save ongoing pieces of work. I use two-pocket folders and put a green sticker on one side to indicate work in progress and a red sticker on the other side to indicate work that is finished.

The primary goal of a writer is to communicate a message. I want the children to embrace drawing as an essential tool to communicate their message. This is drawing that has been consciously envisioned as opposed to drawing that is unplanned. Thinking about their idea, talking it through, and planning and then executing their drawing is the foundation upon which we will build future writing skills. There is great power in the transference of an idea from oneself to another, and I want the children to experience that power and be emboldened by it. At the same time, I am also sneaking in a strategy very early on in the year that all the children can use successfully in the weeks to come. There is no way that I can plan and conduct an hour-long writing workshop if I have to respond to every tug of "I don't know how to write." From now on I can say, "Of course you can! Let's see what you are drawing."

FOCUS LESSON | *Writers Draw*

Making Self-Portraits

Purpose | *To think of an idea, envision it, and then transfer it faithfully onto paper*

Lesson | *Model talking through an idea and reproducing it while drawing a self-portrait.*

Student Extension | *Students draw self-portraits.*

The first writing activity of the year is to draw self-portraits. I model how I carefully look at myself in the mirror before I draw my portrait. As I draw, I keep talking and emphasize that my portrait has to be true to life or people will confuse me with someone else. I would, of course, never put in blue eyes like my favorite Disney princess because my own eyes are black! I model how I carefully sort through the crayon colors available to me and choose the one that fits best. I keep a small mirror next to me and invite children to look into it and tell us some details they might choose to put into their pictures. The mirror goes around, and by the time I have it back, the children have articulated out loud some of those details. Thinking out loud makes the students somewhat accountable for the drawings they will eventually produce. I have materials—paper, skin-colored crayons, and regular crayons—out on the tables, and the children get busy. As I walk around, I refer the children to the ideas they had said out loud and emphasize how they need to be true to the details. *Details* quickly becomes a catchphrase in our room.

I invite the children to write their name on sentence strips, and we put these portraits and the corresponding names around the room. ♜

FOCUS LESSON · *Writers Tell Stories and Hold On to Story Ideas*

Purpose | *To recognize that all of us have many stories to tell of things we like to do or are experts in*

Lesson | *Model drawing a picture of yourself engaged in a favorite activity and make a list of story ideas with the students.*

Student Extension | *Students refer to the list when they need to find a topic to write about.*

"Writers tell stories," I tell the children. "They tell stories about things they know lots about. When you know lots about something, people call you an expert on that subject. You are also experts on many things." I invite the children to share their individual areas of expertise. I quickly find out that Moria is an expert on her mom and dad; Elijah, Cameron, and Daniel are experts on playing; Brian and Kayleigh are experts on bird watching; Jasmine is an expert in ballet; Min Jae is an expert on eating with chopsticks; and Emma and Meghan are experts on taking care of little sisters and brothers!

Besides the ideas we already have, I emphasize that we are also all experts on ourselves—nobody knows more things about us than we do. When I write about myself, I can choose to share any one particular thing about myself that I feel like writing about. I can share what I like to do, for instance, or what I can do really well or what I dislike doing. I share that I am an expert in dancing and then I model how I can draw a picture of myself engaged in dancing and write a few words about it. I ask the children to illustrate their ideas, and we make a class book that includes all our work.

We build up a list of things we might write about later since I want students to know that writers hold on to story ideas that they can later write about. We display it prominently in our classroom. This list includes ideas such as

- Myself
- My family
- My friends
- My pets
- What I like to do
- What I don't like to do
- Special times (birthdays, holidays)
- Favorite things (books, toys, games, cuddly pillows)
- What I can do really well

I tell the children that we can refer to this list when we need story ideas. ♜

Writers Think of Ideas

Making All About Me Books

Purpose   *To think through all that they know about a particular topic before they share with others*

Lesson   *Demonstrate how writers fill themselves up with ideas before writing about a topic in the same way a balloon is completely filled up with air. Model an* All About Me *book.*

Student Extension   *Students make* All About My Family *and* All About Kindergarten *books*

I tell the children that writers need to fill themselves up with ideas before they write. I look through the list we have made of possible writing ideas and announce that I am going to write about myself. I hold up a balloon and puff it up a little bit and share how I could tell people only one thing about myself. The children suggest that I puff it up a bit more and tell some more. I do so and continue doing so till I have shared four to five things about myself. I tell the children that the puffed-up balloon is like my mind when it is filled up with ideas. I deliberately use a simple refrain that is easy for the children to copy, like talking about things I like to do and drawing them on separate sheets of blank paper that I then staple together. I ask for volunteers to share stories about themselves, following the same pattern. Before each child comes up to speak, I blow up the balloon and suggest he or she fill his or her mind with ideas before speaking. As the child speaks, I keep blowing air into the balloon until it is puffed up completely.

To further elaborate on the idea of writing about ourselves, I ask the children to complete accordion books titled *All About Me* at home with their parents. The books have several blank pages with a line of text at the bottom, starting with "When I was 1 . . ." and so on until "When I was 5 . . ." In an accompanying letter to the parents, I suggest using real photographs or hand-drawn pictures and writing some brief text to go with them. As the books are returned to the classroom, I display them and we take turns reading about each other. I find that the children often read these books during independent reading time and we get to know each other and find connections as a community.

"My family likes to . . ." pages

The children and I make books about our families and about school. The books are already stapled, and we work on a page a day, choosing an idea and drawing a picture. The family books are based on a song that we made up titled "I Am in a Family," sung to the tune of "The Muffin Man." Each page has a blank space for a drawing and a partial line of the refrain that writers complete ("My family likes to . . ."). I read *The Twelve Days of Kindergarten* by Deborah Lee Rose and Carey Armstrong-Ellis as a model for our kindergarten books. Each page in these books too has a space to draw and space to write that follows a refrain ("In kindergarten, I . . ."). The children think of different things they do in the classroom, draw a picture, and add some words as they complete this book.

Each day, I conduct a focus lesson in which I model choosing an idea, drawing a picture with lots of details, and writing the best I can. Within two to three weeks, my students begin to get a sense of the writing process as a process that records ideas and happenings in pictures and words. ♜

BUILDING STRATEGIES TO WRITE WORDS

I slowly introduce word-solving strategies to my class as we make our books. The strategies taught in these focus lessons form anchor charts and use the same icons as in the charts for reading.

STRATEGIES	MODELING
Writers sound words out.	I offer alphabet charts to the children that they place in their writing folders. The same chart is displayed in a larger size in the classroom. I demonstrate the strategy of saying a word, hearing the sounds, writing the letters that match, rereading, and writing some more.
Writers write quick-and-easy words.	I model using the word wall and the laminated rainbow-fish charts that have the sight words displayed on them. There are several copies of the charts in the baskets that hold all the writing supplies.

Writers write words they recognize.	As we work on our kindergarten books, I model how I use words around the room to write. The children and I brainstorm how we may use the center labels, the schedule, and other displays to retrieve words we need.
Writers write words from dictionaries.	I model using picture dictionaries to find words we need.
Writers write words the best they can.	I model how sometimes we just have to keep on going and problem solve using a combination of the strategies we already know.
Writers reread to check their writing.	I demonstrate how to keep spaces between my words so that others can read my writing.

FOCUS LESSON | *Writers Write for Different Purposes*

Making Signs

Purpose   To open up writing possibilities for students by inviting them to explore writing for different purposes—to name, to label, to define, and to categorize

Lesson   Model writing and illustrating a sign for a classroom area.

Student Extension   Students make signs and labels for different areas of the classroom. They can simply label the area or list materials found in that area and can also make specific recommendations for the use of the space.

I open up writing possibilities for my children as I invite them to share in unpacking materials and arranging the room to define work and play spaces. I model making signs, lists, and labels and later model writing messages. Signs made by the children quickly spring up around the room.

Daniel's sign

Meghan's sign

Daniel makes a sign with a simple rule for the construction area: "Don't break others' things." There is an accompanying picture of a child weeping because his Lego construction has been destroyed.

Jasmine makes a sign for the writing area that admonishes one to concentrate while writing.

Meghan makes a sign for our meeting area: "Keep your magic. It is the best. I hope you do that." "Magic" refers to our class rule of keeping one's hands, feet, and bodies to oneself and respecting each other's space. I am very grateful as Meghan hands me this sign to display in the meeting area, as shifting attentions often result in sneaky invasions of a friend's space, and we all know how that can totally disrupt whole-group lessons. ♜

Writing About Events That Really Happened to Us

Personal Narratives

Purpose *To recognize that writing is a process through which we can record stories before they get lost forever*

Lesson *Model a personal narrative based on a shared experience that you have had with the class. Build the text with the help of the children.*

Student Extension *Students write their own personal narratives.*

I normally model my first personal narrative on a shared experience that I have had with my class. There are obviously many instances to choose from, but I like to choose one that is memorable and humorous. I gather the children and tell them that I want to write about this event that really happened to me or my story will be lost forever. I talk aloud about the event as I draw and add details to make it seem real. Since the children are familiar with the event, they remind me of details that I may need to put in, like the color of the dress I was wearing or who was near me at that time or what the expression on my face was.

So far, the materials we have used for writing have been blank sheets of paper or premade booklets. We have spent the major part of our time concentrating on drawing and adding some words. I now introduce a new kind of paper that is mostly blank but has a line to write some text at the bottom. I ask the children to help me add a sentence to make my story complete. We make up the sentence together, and the children and I problem solve letters and sounds as I write it out.

The children start generating their own writing topics based on something that actually happened to them. At this stage the majority still concentrate on immediate events. Each day we meet as a group and I model my own story. I then ask the children to share their ideas of what they might write about, and as they do, we add to our collective pool of writing possibilities.

As a group, we review what we know good writers do and go over the list we already have on one of our anchor charts. I have made a writing-process chart that shows the stages of writing—thinking of an idea, drawing a picture, writing words, adding details, and sharing—and also has an area to indicate a need for help. I pass out little laminated cards in the

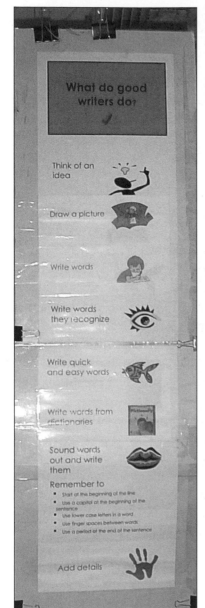

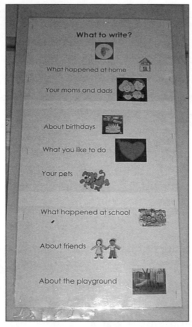

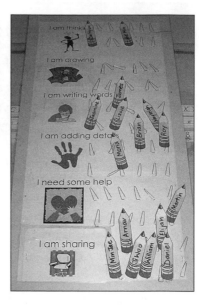

Writing Strategies anchor charts

shape of pencils with the children's names on them and demonstrate how the children can move through the writing process on the chart by sticking their pencil onto the corresponding area. This chart is helpful as I begin to confer around the room. I can see at a glance the stage each child is at and can also immediately begin to help those who have indicated that they need help as we transition from our daily focus lesson to independent writing. ♜

Telling the Story Over Your Fingers

Purpose	*To move from recording solitary events to developing a story sequence*
Lesson	*Demonstrate the strategy of telling a story over one's fingers to aid the development of a story sequence.*
Student Extension	*Students use five-page booklets to develop their own stories.*

I want to move from recording single events to developing a story. I gather the children around me and confide that the strangest thing happened to me this morning as I was about to make breakfast. I had decided to make pancakes at the last minute and got everything ready, but when I opened the refrigerator to get some eggs out, the egg container was empty! I finally had to have plain, boring old cereal for breakfast.

I tell the children that my idea is too big to fit onto one page and so I need to spread it out over several pages. That is not going to be easy, as I may lose track of what to write and draw on each page. I announce that I am going to use a special trick to help me do this—I am going to tell it over my five fingers. I close my hand in a fist and put out my thumb as I start my story. I put out each finger as I tell a bit more. As I get toward my ring finger, I exclaim that I had better come to the end of my story or I will run out of fingers!

Jasmine's story: "My shipment got flooded."

"My family was opening our boxes."

"And then me and my sister had to throw away some toys."

"'When I Got My Dog' by Kimi"

"I got my dog outside the fence."

"My dog was brown."

"We brought my dog home."

"My dog went upstairs and pooped."

"My dog went to the vet."

I have little five-page booklets ready for the children. The pages are blank with a line for text at the bottom. I demonstrate how I am going to illustrate my story over the five pages by remembering how I told it over my five fingers. I talk as I draw. I save adding words for another day. I ask the children whether they have some stories they'd like to tell over my five fingers and hold my fist out and ask them to come and open it to bring their stories to life.

Jasmine has recently moved and she writes about waiting for her container to arrive. Unfortunately there was some flooding during the move, and she and her sister had to throw away many of their toys! Kimi writes a story about how her whole family went to choose a dog from the pound. They picked out a brown dog and then all piled into the car and came back home with broad smiles on their faces. She ends her story by talking about how the dog pooped on the staircase as soon as they got home and they had to take him to the vet!

Arnav writes about being sad while saying goodbye to his father as he left on a trip. The story is a perfect excuse for drawing his favorite object, fantastically detailed airplanes! When asked to complete his story, Arnav draws the many presents his father brought back for him when he returned.

The icon for adding details on our writing-process chart is five fingers. I encourage the children to move their laminated name cards to the area indicated by this icon during independent writing over the course of the next two weeks. Every day, after my demonstration, I invite a few children to tell their story over my five fingers. We proceed to demonstrating a story over the fingers of a friend's hand and also over one's own hand so that the children have abundant practice in stretching out their stories in the form of a narrative. ♟

FOCUS LESSON — *Outside and Inside Stories*

Purpose   *To show how a writer can add feelings and thoughts about events to create interest*

Lesson   *Demonstrate that once the story events have been told over five fingers, the fist is opened to reveal inner thoughts about the events.*

Student Extension   *Students add their thoughts as they write their own stories.*

Once we all have a sense of an unfolding narrative, I explain how storytellers don't share just the event but also their thoughts about the event. I remind the children about our five-finger strategy and tell them that the sequence of events tells the "outside" of a story. Now that our fist is

Five-finger strategy

opened, we also need to tell the reader about the "inside" of our story, which includes our thoughts at the time, our feelings, and our opinions, and the thoughts, feelings, and opinions of others.

Besides the prestapled booklets, the materials at the writing center include blank sheets that the children can staple together to form their own booklets according to the number of pages they need. I also fit in a focus lesson on how you need only three staples on the left side—top, middle, and bottom—to hold your booklet together, not fifty million staples placed randomly everywhere! ♜

WRITERS SEND STORIES OUT INTO THE WORLD

Each day at the end of writing workshop, I invite a few children to share their work from the Author's Chair. The writing-process chart keeps this system streamlined and effective. I encourage the children to place their laminated name cards in the area that indicates they are ready to share. After the first few children share, we move the other cards up in line. More children add their cards to the line over the course of the week. There is usually no dearth of authors willing to share! The ones who have already shared that week have to wait their turn till next week.

Sharing from the
Author's Chair

As we share our stories, we work on specific strategies like author behavior, audience behavior, asking questions, making suggestions, and making comments.

I explain to the children that writers send their stories out into the world so that others can read them. This process is called publishing. Before we publish, we need to make sure that our pictures and words can be understood by others. For this we need to clean up our writing, following writing conventions and including titles for our stories.

FOCUS LESSON	*Writers Follow Writing Conventions*
Purpose	*To demonstrate the value of following simple writing conventions like spacing between words*
Lesson	*Through interactive writing lessons, model the practice of using spaces between words to separate one word from another while making class books.*
Student Extension	*Students contribute to class books.*

I write a sentence with no finger spaces and then pretend to reread it, stumbling, frowning, and reading obvious gibberish. I explain that leaving

Class book page by Lizwe: "At AES we are friends."

A AES WeR FRS.

Class book page by Arnav: "There is a playground."

vɑr ES ɑ PLɑ.R.GɐD

finger spaces helps the reader make out different words. We also work on this strategy during our shared and interactive writing. One day every week, we spend our writing workshop time making a class book to which all students contribute a page. During this time, working on the first page interactively while sharing the pen takes the place of a writing focus lesson, and the children help me construct the text by adding ideas and sounding out words. After the interactive writing lesson, each student works on a page independently, following the main idea of the book. I generally work on community themes through our class books, which are about our classmates, our school, our school custodians, the countries we come from, our similarities and differences. Very often our class book is modeled after a picture book that follows a pattern or a Big Book that has a catchy refrain. After reading *The Twelve Days of Kindergarten* or the Big Book version of the popular song *The More We Get Together*, for example, we made our own versions of the text.

To make the best use of the time we have at hand, we work on differences between letters, words, and sentences through our literacy stations. ♜

FOCUS LESSON

Writers Generate Titles for Stories

Making Book Covers

Purpose To learn how to generate titles for stories

Lesson *Demonstrate different ways a writer could plan a title for a story using mentor texts such as* Just Me and My Dad *(writer gives main idea),* The Rainbow Fish *(writer titles the book after the main character),* Franklin Is Bossy *(writer identifies a problem).*

Student Extension *Students create titles and covers for their books.*

I have pulled out several of the books we have been reading during our interactive read-alouds by Marcus Pfister, Paulette Bourgeois, Mercer Mayer, and Kevin Henkes. I hold up a book by each author and comment on the book cover. I wonder aloud at the authors' title choices and why they chose to illustrate the cover the way they did. The stories are familiar to the children, and we quickly brainstorm a list of possible ideas for making a title, including the following:

- Give the main idea of the story (*Just Me and My Dad*).
- Use the main character's name (*The Rainbow Fish*, *Chrysanthemum*).
- State the problem (*Franklin Is Bossy*).

I pass out the books to the children and ask them to share other things they notice on the book covers. The children all see that each cover carries the author's name and the illustration matches the story. They also notice that the cover is made up of a different material than the rest of the book. This last observation caught me unprepared the first time it was made. The children wanted to illustrate their own covers once we had built our shared understanding of what constitutes a book cover. When I handed out regular paper, they protested that it was the same kind as the rest of their book and therefore unsuitable! I had not stocked up on card stock that first time and, red-faced, had to rush out and borrow from a neighboring classroom. Now I always make sure I have enough card stock to satisfy the justifiable necessity of designing a cover that looks and feels different from the rest of the book. Once we have a common understanding of how we could design a cover, the children then make covers for their own books. ♜

Writers Share wth Audiences and Celebrate Writing

Purpose   To learn how to comment on writing

Lesson   *Explain that we can comment on the writing of others by offering positive feedback, asking for clarification, or making suggestions for change and that those comments are meant to be supportive.*

Student Extension   *Students read the stories of their classmates and comment on them.*

By the end of the first trimester, we have several personal narratives that we have written and one that we have chosen to publish. We are ready for our first writing celebration. I prop up the books by the children on separate easels around the room. I keep a stack of index cards and pencils near each book and invite the children to walk around and read each other's stories. Once they've read a story, they have to write a comment on an index card and tuck it under the easel. I emphasize that the comments have to be positive. The children are used to commenting, questioning, and suggesting changes to stories by their peers during our daily Author's Chair. This time they have to write their thoughts down instead of saying them out loud.

The room hums quietly as the children walk around and read. Most of the stories are familiar, as we have worked through the process of writing them as a community. The comments are unstintingly joyous.

Meghan's letter to Michelle

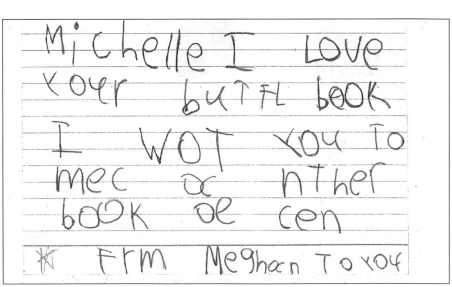

Meghan's letter to Michelle says, "I love your beautiful book. I want you to make another book the same." Echoing Meghan's sentiment, I too want us to continue to make similar books, and yet other books as well—books that tell stories from our lives, of who we are and what is important to us over the course of the year. Like Meghan, I too want us to make other books just the same! ♜

4

LET THE SHOW BEGIN!

Going from the known to the new builds a solid foundation for any learner. We start our kindergarten year with literacy experiences that the children are or can become most comfortable with. The letters in the individual names of the children open up the world of alphabets, letters, and words for them. Reading stories that reflect familiar incidents enable my kindergartners to put themselves in the shoes of the character and form intimate and sometimes surprising connections leading to deeper comprehension. We write about what we know best or are an expert at through personal narratives that have an embedded story structure and sequence. The transition to fairy tales is a logical scaffold. Fairy tales tend to have strong, predictable structures and lend themselves to repeated opportunities for students to interact with the texts and apply retelling and comprehension strategies, enabling them to transfer these strategies to other text structures. Fairy tales also lend themselves to performance that can be incorporated within the learning community throughout the year.

The children and I get ready to expand our reading and writing workshop by exploring fairy tales. We immerse ourselves in stories, discussing well-loved titles and authors. Our classroom library grows bigger every day as I invite the children to bring in their favorite books from home. These include books in their native languages, and the children and I marvel at how these stories look familiar, although they are in different languages with different illustrations. As a class, we discuss how we are able to know the story of *Sleeping Beauty* or *Cinderella* and retell it even though we can't read the words in another language. The children tell me that they know through the pictures. This stresses the importance of keeping one's mind alive to the messages carried through illustrations for some of the strong readers in my class, one of whom had confidently stated that only babies look at the pictures to figure out the story! The children also tell me that they can predict the story because they've heard it before, and I share that that is one of the most important reading strategies that I rely on personally as well.

Some of the books, while similar to familiar stories in English, incorporate local cultures and customs. *Lon Po Po* by Ed Young, while similar to *Red Riding Hood*, is a Chinese version of this popular fairy tale and is very clearly set in China. Michelle, who is from Taiwan, explains things to me and her friends as I read the book, and we all feel indebted to her as she brings her personal knowledge of the culture to our classroom and enriches our understanding of the story.

EXPANDING THE READING WORKSHOP

The focus lessons that follow guide us through the different stages for expanding the reading workshop. The children explore the genre of fairy tales in depth and learn to identify its characteristics.

FOCUS LESSON	*Readers Picture Stories in Their Minds*

Purpose — *To recall images in our minds—of characters, settings, and scenes—and represent them through a drawing to recreate a similar image in the mind of an audience*

Lesson — *Model thinking of a favorite story, deliberating about how best to represent it through a picture before actually drawing it.*

Student Extension — *Students draw pictures of their favorite stories.*

I sit surrounded by popular fairy-tale books: *Cinderella, Sleeping Beauty, Goldilocks and the Three Bears, Rumpelstiltskin, The Little Red Hen, The Three Billy Goats Gruff, Jack and the Beanstalk, Snow White and the Seven Dwarves, The Gingerbread Man, Tom Thumb,* and *Red Riding Hood.* We have been reading them this past week, and the children have chimed in whenever they've come across familiar ones. Today, I hold up each book and talk briefly about the story. When I ask the kids whether they have any favorites, the class erupts in a clamor of voices. I then ask them whether they think they all like the same one, and the answer is a vehement "no." To make their preference clearer, I tell them they can draw a picture of their favorite story and write its title out to display around our classroom.

I model how I would make an illustration of my favorite story, thinking aloud for a minute and pondering over my decision. I tell the children that it is very hard for me to choose. I love so many stories! However, *Cinderella* is one of my absolute favorites, as I love the idea of a fairy godmother granting wishes. When my decision is made, I take a large sheet of white watercolor paper and talk aloud as I draw, telling the children that I have to be careful with my drawing so that it is absolutely clear that my choice is *Cinderella* and not just any other princess story. I'd better put in the glass slippers, I announce, as well as the fairy godmother and her wand. Maybe drawing the castle in the background would help identify the story as well. I quickly sketch, making sure that I am including all the details that I have been talking about, and then demonstrate how I can copy the title from the cover of the book.

We pass out large sheets of watercolor paper and permanent markers. I remind the children to be conscious of their choice and to take a minute to decide. Some children begin to draw immediately, while others take a moment to look through the books in our library and deliberate about their choice. After drawing, they fill in their pictures with vibrant watercolors. Ido, who is from Israel, tells me that his favorite story is not in our library but that he has seen it in a movie. This prompts a lively discussion on how stories are found in places other than books. I invite him to draw his representation of the movie he has seen, and he happily gets to work.

We gather together for a share at the end. In a circle, the children hold their paintings up and talk about the stories they've chosen. We realize that as a class we know a lot of different stories, and we also begin to get a glimmer of how stories are similar and different. ♜

Cinderella *by Kayleigh*

FOCUS LESSON

Stories Have Beginnings, Middles, and Ends

Purpose   *To identify the beginning, middle, and end of a story and to view a story as an unfolding narrative sequence*

Lesson   *Talk about the narrative sequence of a favorite story; then on the separate sections of a Beginning, Middle, and End sheet (see Appendix), draw out the sequence and write a brief sentence about each section.*

Student Extension   *Students identify and draw the three sections of their favorite stories.*

I show the children the illustration that I made of my favorite story in the previous lesson and tell them that I will try to retell it to them in words. I deliberately keep the retelling very sparse, mixing up the beginning, the middle, and the end. The children protest loudly and correct my mistakes as I retell it. I ask them where I was going wrong. Brian indignantly tells me that I was mixing up all the parts and that made the story very mixed up. "Aha! Brian, does that mean that stories have parts?" "Of course," he replies confidently. I hand out his illustration and ask him to retell his favorite story, assuring him that I am sure he will do a better job than I.

Brian faces his friends and retells his story, *The Gingerbread Man*. "The mom was baking the gingerbread man and then the gingerbread man ran away," begins Brian's recount. He ends his story by telling us that the fox ate up the gingerbread man. Soon, other children want a turn. We do a couple more retellings, and then I explain that everyone will get a chance to retell their story.

I show the Beginning, Middle, and End sheet and model how I would fill out each section with pictures and words. We pass out the sheets and the illustrations the children made of their favorite stories. We work on the sheets a couple of days, as there is a writing component as well as drawing. At the end of each session, I invite a few children to share.

When I look over the completed sheets, I find that there is a range of comprehension about the narrative sequence of a story. There are some children who have almost a complete grasp of this division, like Min Jae, who is retelling *The Rainbow Fish*. In the beginning section, she writes, "The little fish came to the rainbow fish. Can I have some scales? No, said the rainbow fish." In the middle, "The rainbow fish talked to the starfish." In the end, "The octopus said to share his scales." Others like Kayleigh are beginning to get a sense of how stories work but are still focused on the smaller problems within the story. Kayleigh is retelling *Cinderella*, and in the beginning section she writes, "Cinderella is dreaming she wanted to go to the ball." In the middle, "The fairy godmother came and gave her wish." In the end, "Cinderella left her glass slipper."

Looking over the children's work gives me an idea of the direction I want to take over the next few days, the pace that I need to set for my instruction, and the specific children that this instruction will need to target. I know that we will need to keep refining our collective understanding of the parts that make up stories through more read-alouds and practice retellings. ♜

Kayleigh's retelling of Cinderella

<table>
<tr><td>In the beginning...</td><td>In the middle...</td><td>In the end...</td></tr>
</table>

In the beginning...	In the middle...	In the end...
SEDRR ALA	THE FARE	SEDRR ALA
IS DEMEM	GOD MAMR	LAFD
SHE WJT	KAM	HR GLAJ
FAE BOL	AND DD WAEP2	

FOCUS LESSON *Stories Have Characters and Settings*

Purpose To *identify the essential components of a story—characters (who is the story about?), place (where is the story set?), and time (when is the story set?)*

Lesson Model *thinking about the separate components of a favorite story and drawing them by using the Parts of a Story 1 sheet (see Appendix).*

Student Extension Students *draw parts of their favorite story.*

We gather in the meeting area, and I tell the children that I am very proud of the way they are becoming such experts on stories. "But we were already experts on writing about stories from our lives," says Roy. "These stories are different, Roy," chimes in Jasmine. "They are pretend." I reiterate Jasmine's opinion and tell the class that today we will learn something more about how stories work.

I show them the Parts of a Story 1 sheet and tell them that stories always need to have characters and a place or places, and that they are set in a time. Going back to my favorite story, I model how I would separate the parts and invite the children to do the same. We share our story parts at the end of the session. ♖

Parts of a Story 1: Cinderella

FOCUS LESSON | *Stories Have Problems*

Purpose

To understand that stories can't be straight lines. A story curve is created when characters encounter a problem and then try to solve it. Stories work because of this problem/solution dynamic.

Lesson

Model thinking about the central problem in a favorite story by using the Parts of a Story 2 sheet (see Appendix).

Student Extension

Students try to identify and write about the central problem of their favorite story.

I read aloud *Cinderella* to the class. "Was there a problem in the story?" I ask the children. "She wanted to go to the ball," "Her wicked stepmother was mean to her," "She lost her slipper," "She didn't have any clothes to go to the party," "She didn't listen to the fairy"—all these differing responses display a beginning understanding of how problems in stories are created by the author.

I chart all the answers, and then as a class we try to figure out what was the biggest or the central problem. The discussion provokes much thought and talk. I write down the final consensus on my Parts of a Story 2 sheet.

I tell the children that they will need to think back to the stories they were experts on and do what I did to find the biggest problem. I remind them that there may be more than one problem in a story but most often the author would have the thread of the biggest one running throughout the story. I ask them to keep that thread in mind when they dig through their stories to find the main problem.

I pass out the favorite-story illustrations that the children did earlier. I ask them to study their drawings and invite volunteers to break them up into parts just as I did with *Cinderella*. As a group we model a few more stories and then I ask the children to work on their own while I help as needed. I see Min Jae has a fair grasp of the problem in *The Rainbow Fish*. She writes, "The little fish went to the rainbow fish and he said no." And Brian identifies the central problem in *The Gingerbread Man*: "Every person wanted to eat him."

Problem?
AVREPRJIN   WOTTOETHIM

Parts of a Story 2: Brian's example

Kayleigh has worked really hard with her recounting and retelling and now talks of the beginning, middle, and end in far broader terms than she did earlier, but her focus on the finer details sometimes makes her miss the central problem. About Cinderella, she writes that the problem was "the stepsister ripped all her dresses."

Problem?
THE STAP SESTRS
REPT OXL A F HRDAS

Parts of a Story 2: Kayleigh's example

Jasmine also focuses on one event in her story, "Jasmine and Raja." She writes that the problem was that "Jasmine wanted to run away but her father didn't let her." ♖

FOCUS LESSON

Stories Have Solutions to Problems

Purpose

To recognize two things: (1) solutions to problems in stories are always worked out within the story itself and never occur at random or outside the text, and (2) a special characteristic of fairy tales is that characters often encounter problems three times before actually resolving them.

Lesson

Model thinking about the solution to the problem in a favorite story through the Parts of a Story 2 sheet.

Student Extension

Students identify and write about how problems in their favorite stories get resolved.

As a class we review what we know about fairy tales from our daily read-aloud. Several hands wave madly in the air as the children eagerly wait their turn to share their developing knowledge of how fairy tales work. Brian, with his precocious vocabulary, shares, "Fairy tales were probably written a long time ago, but we don't know who the real authors are. A lot of them begin with 'Once upon a time.'" Josiah tags on to that statement, "They are not real stories. They have magic in them," and Emma adds, "All fairy tales have characters." Cameron shares, "They happen in places like castles. I am going to write about a knight in a castle during writing workshop." I note that Cameron is already thinking of applying his awareness of this new genre to his writing, and I congratulate him for having a plan for later on that day.

Our discussion takes on a new focus as Josiah shares that events in fairy tales often happen in "threes." I ask him to expand on that thought, and he explains that he has observed that in a lot of his favorite stories, like *Goldilocks and the Three Bears, Jack and the Beanstalk*, and *The Three Billy Goats Gruff*, the problem recurred three times before it got solved. I mentally dance a little jig at the perfect segue that Josiah has given us into our focus lesson for the day.

I ask the class whether they'd noticed something similar while they were trying to figure out what the problem was in their favorite stories, and several children nod assent. We clarify this thinking as a group by looking through the books Josiah referred to and retelling the problem and the number of times the character attempted to solve it before finally succeeding. I tell the class that repeating a problem three times is a particular trick of the author to make the story more interesting. I remind them of our previous discussion about story problems and ask them whether they can think of how the problem got solved in their chosen stories.

I model finding the solution to the problem I had identified on my Parts of a Story 2 sheet for *Cinderella* and writing it down and then hand out the children's sheets for them to complete. I notice that Min Jae, while writing about *The Rainbow Fish*, writes, "He had scales and he was angry. Later they shared the scales," and I know that she is still unclear about which is the problem and which is the solution. Kayleigh, who was writing about *Cinderella*, writes that the problem was solved by "the fairy godmother and she made her another dress." Jasmine writes that the problem in her story was solved when "in the night she ran away."

I know I will need to model sifting through a story to find its central problem and to discover the solution a few more times before the children grasp this concept completely. I continue to model as I read aloud every day. The children also share their completed sheets, a few at a time, with the group as they finish. With suggestions and comments from their friends and me, our collective understanding becomes clearer. ♜

THE SHOW BEGINS

During our writing workshop, we have been busy creating beautiful sceneries that hang from the ceiling in our meeting area and are set up in such a way as to create a space for performance with room for an audience. (See Chapter 5.) We are now ready to begin exploring comprehension strategies such as visualizing and inferring in greater depth.

We use the same sign-up system for this area that I established at the beginning of the year; it is one that I continue to add to through the rest of our time together. In addition to the different areas in the classroom such as dramatic play; building and construction; listening centers; Big Books; classroom library; writing, math, and science centers, we have an area designated for storytelling with props. Crowded here are masks of different animals that can be used to act out many of the Big Books we've used in our shared reading. The entire cast of animals making an appearance in *Mrs. Wishy-Washy* are frankly a little ragged around the edges because of their popularity! I also stock this area with simple headbands that I make that can be used interchangeably to represent different characters. I make color copies of these characters from our Big Books, laminate them, and attach Velcro to the backs. I laminate headbands and add Velcro tabs to them as well. The children can choose a character picture and attach it to their headband and, lo and behold, they are suddenly a Meanie from *The Meanies* or Huggles from *Huggles Can Juggle*. There are also character necklaces that have a laminated picture of a popular character on a string that the children can place around their necks to attain a different identity as well as finger puppets and hand puppets that can be used to retell stories. It is in this area where our sceneries now hang. I add feather boas and spangly capes, swirling skirts and swashbuckling helmets, magic wands and knights' armor.

Earlier in the year, when the children used this area to act out stories from Big Books, I would invite them to sign up, applying, as always, our usual four-to-six-people quota in an area. I would then invite one child to be the narrator, in charge of reading the Big Book and controlling the pacing of the story. The rest of the children could choose different roles and costume themselves appropriately. We would then retell the story through dramatic interpretation. The performers didn't invent dialogue at this stage; they could, however, invest their character with the qualities and characteristics they deemed fit and say the dialogue denoted in the text. The narrator would read all the other parts. Our performers never lacked for an audience to applaud their efforts, and this area has always been among the most popular in the classroom. Newly stocked and newly decorated, this area looks even more appealing though the terms of usage remain the same, and I anticipate a smooth transition into storytelling and performing a new genre.

FOCUS LESSON — *Readers Envision Characters, Settings, and Actions*

Purpose   *To truly experience the world of a story by walking in the shoes of a character and trying to imagine how that character would walk, talk, and behave*

Lesson   *Direct a performance of a well-known fairy tale with a small group. Help children choose roles and discuss how performers can experience the world of the character by thinking about how the character would act in a particular situation, keeping in mind that different characters would behave in different ways. Finally, after discussing the story sequence, keep the performance moving along through narration.*

Student Extension   *Students perform different well-known fairy tales.*

I invite children to sign up in our redecorated storytelling center as they arrive in the morning. I gather my group together in the meeting area and explain that we are going to try to perform a story in the new genre of fairy tales that we have been exploring. We choose a story that they know very well, *Rumpelstiltskin*. I hold up the book, and I also hold up the Parts of a Story 2 sheet that I've made about the story to clarify the main problem and its solution. I remind the group that to make the story clear, we have to make sure to follow the right sequence. As this is our first attempt, I am going to focus on a skill that the children already have some practice with, retelling, and a newer one, walking in the shoes of the characters in a story.

I ask the children to choose the characters they wish to play. There is some amount of negotiation; naturally, all the children have specific ideas about which of the roles are important and of course nobody wants to be the "bad guy." I explain that stories can work only if all characters do their part, and they make their final choices. I tell the children that our storytelling today is going to be a little bit different from our earlier experience of storytelling and performance. Then, when we retold *Mrs. Wishy-Washy*, for instance, we were following the text or script from a book while the narrator read the parts in between. This time round, the narrator is going to keep the story moving along, but the actors have to imagine and decide how their characters should walk and talk and behave. By doing this, we better understand the story and also enjoy it more. I explain that the author gives us lots of clues about the characters and if we are careful readers, we can use those clues to imagine what the characters would do and think and feel even though the author does not specifically tell us.

As we get ready to perform, I watch as Jasmine transforms herself into a regal princess by straightening her shoulders, Brian rushes off to find his cape that he'd brought in today since he had a feeling he would need it, Ido decides to invest his wicked elf with a ferocious scowl, and Cameron stands tall as the knight. The children make up the dialogue as they go along, and I keep the story going as the narrator. We do a practice run, and then we are ready to perform before an audience.

I ask the rest of the class if they want to watch the performance and quickly discuss audience expectations even as the performers hide behind the scenes they've chosen for themselves, giggling with excitement. There is something magical about a story coming to life like this, and I can see the engagement of both the performers and the audience in the story that is so familiar, yet imbued now with the imaginations of these little storytellers. We repeat this process over the next few days, performing different stories with different groups till all my students have had a chance to perform. ♟

FOCUS LESSON — Readers Imagine Dialogues

Purpose   *To experience the world of a story by imagining what a character would say and how he or she would say it, and to recognize that characters act in unique and special ways and that their speech and movement are often clues to their inner thoughts and feelings*

Lesson   *Read* The Enormous Watermelon *and model how different characters would speak and act as they come over to help Old Mother Hubbard, the main character, pull out the gigantic watermelon from her garden.*

Student Extension   *Students choose a fairy-tale or nursery-rhyme character to represent, draw a picture, and insert dialogue for that character as he or she helps Old Mother Hubbard.*

Over the course of the next few weeks, our storytelling area continues to be immensely popular. The children use it independently, needing minimal supervision. I no longer have to play narrator since the day Meghan picked up the book her group had chosen and confidently turned the pages, reading the story through its illustrations. Meghan was such a great role model that now other children step forward to play narrator. I think they realize that they then control the story, a very powerful feeling indeed! I am part of the audience every day as I enjoy our regular impromptu performances.

I now would like the children to become more conscious of dialogue and focus on it in relation to particular characters. We read *The Enormous Watermelon*, a spin on the popular story *The Great Big Turnip*. In the story, several nursery-rhyme characters come to help Old Mother Hubbard pull her enormous watermelon out of her garden patch. By now we are familiar with a whole cast of fairy-tale and nursery-rhyme characters. I ask the children who else could have helped Mother Hubbard, and the children come up with several ideas. "Would all the characters speak and act in the same way?" I wonder. "If I were Cinderella, I would ask the fairy godmother to help," says Jasmine. Kayleigh giggles and pretends she is Sleeping Beauty: "I am so tired and sleepy!" Roy, our champion performer of any mouse parts, declares, "I am too little to pull the watermelon, but I can help eat it!"

I ask the children if they'd like to make a class book patterned after the book we've just read, and the children choose their favorite characters from a list that we brainstormed during writing workshop. I remind them to be mindful of their characters before they draw and write dialogue on the large sheets of paper—blank except for a speech bubble—that I provide. We gather for a share, and the children take on the roles of their chosen characters. I close the lesson by reminding them to keep their ears open for dialogue during their independent reading or when I read aloud to them. I also ask them to continue using it in their story performances. ♜

FOCUS LESSON | *Readers Use Expression When They Tell a Story*

Purpose

To see that when we invest a character's dialogue or action with expression, we convey our impression of the story and also influence how a listener perceives the story

Lesson

Demonstrate the difference expression—not just what the characters say but how they say it—makes to the entire story experience.

Student Extension

Students practice investing characters with expression.

The children are such natural actors that performing has become an extension of playing in our classroom. Meanwhile, we also carry on with the other components of our reading program—reading aloud, independent reading, and shared reading. The classroom library is a popular site as the children hunt for books they would like to reread or perform. It is very common to see small groups of children sprawled around a book discussing characters, events, or dialogues.

I want the children to use expression now. As we gather together for our read-aloud, I share a story about my daughter, who liked me to read to her even when she was a fluent reader herself. When asked why, she had told me, "It's because you do 'impressions,' Mama." I had laughed and said, "You mean expressions, don't you?" Later, I realized that *impressions* was probably not such an inaccurate word. When we invest a character's dialogue or action with expression, we convey our impression of the story and also influence how a listener perceives the story.

I demonstrate reading without expression by reading today's story in a bland monotone. Amidst a clamor of protests, I have to stop. "You can't do that. This is boring. You have to enter the story, remember?" Brian reminds me.

I start reading again, expressively this time, and there is an audible sigh of relief. As we finish, I remind the children not to forget expression when they tell their stories to their partners after independent reading is over. ♜

FOCUS LESSON *Readers Imagine Between Picture Scenes*

Purpose   *To recognize that when readers imagine what goes on in between scenes, they can try to predict what may happen next*

Lesson   *Repeat the performance of a familiar fairy tale. During the second performance, stop and think about what the characters may be doing in between scenes and incorporate that into the narrative.*

Student Extension   *Students incorporate between-scene moments into their performance of fairy tales.*

We are watching a performance of *The Three Little Pigs* by our ever-spontaneous cast of storytellers. After the show I tell the children that, as a reader, my mind keeps spinning within the story even when the author stops writing about a particular event. I wonder what the characters do in between events—where they go, what they think, who they meet. When I do this, I enter the story with my thoughts, and then I can predict what is going to happen next. I invite volunteers to perform the story again, this time imagining what the little pigs do in between scenes. I tell the audience that for today's lesson, they can give suggestions to the performers so that we can all pretend to enter the story together.

The second performance is a very noisy, vigorous production imbued with much more dialogue, action, and side stories than the first one, as we are all thinking and acting like readers who are in the story. ♜

Readers Predict What Is Going to Happen Next

Purpose

To make predictions based on their knowledge of the story (text clues) together with their own personal background knowledge

Lesson

Read Dream Snow *and model how a reader can predict events by carefully following text clues and matching them up with one's own background knowledge.*

Student Extension

Students contribute a page toward a class book that suggests an alternate ending for Dream Snow.

We talk about predicting what's going to happen next in the story as a natural extension of our daily read-aloud. Today I focus on this strategy in particular. We read *Dream Snow* by Eric Carle, a story that is already familiar to the children, and then I ask them whether they remember the time I had talked about carrying on with the story in my head even after I stop reading. When I see several heads nod, I tell them that today we will try thinking about the story even after the last page.

The story we have just read is a very simple one. A farmer has several animals that he names One, Two, Three, Four, and Five. One cold night, while the farmer is sleeping, he dreams of a huge snowfall covering his farm and all his animals. The children have to guess the animals by observing the shape of the snow on top of each animal. When the farmer wakes, he looks out into a magical snow-covered landscape. Dressed in a very familiar fur-lined, warm, red snowsuit, he hurries out with a sack and sets up presents under a tree, near the barn. He decorates the tree for Christmas and yells out, "Merry Christmas to all!"

"I wonder what is in those presents. Who are they for?" I muse out loud. The children come up with several ideas. "A puppy, I think it is a puppy!" exclaims Ellali. "No, I think the presents are for the animals. Look, the farmer is looking at them. I think he'll give the horse a blanket," says Brian, who usually follows pictures and words very carefully when he listens to a story. "Wow, Brian! I can see that you are really thinking from the clues in the story. But can you explain why you think the horse would need a blanket?" I ask. "Well, I have seen horses with blankets before, and I think he looks cold in the picture, and so I thought that if I was the farmer, I would give him a blanket," responds Brian. "So what you did was put together what you knew about the story and about horses and then you put yourself in place of the farmer and came up with your answer," I say, clarifying Brian's strategy for the rest of the class. "I wonder if anyone else can do what you just did."

At this time, I briefly consider whether I should introduce the word *inference* or just let the discussion continue. I go with the second option even though I know my kids love the thought of a special word to describe what they are doing. Several more ideas are suggested, all clearly demonstrating that the children have caught on to the idea that random ideas will not find favor with their peers as much as well-considered ones that follow leads offered by the author. At the end of the discussion, I reinforce the strategy and stress that good readers always notice the clues given by the author and put that together with their personal background knowledge to guess events within and without the story. ♜

FOCUS LESSON   *Readers Ask Questions*

Purpose

To ask questions within the text (about story events or about character actions and motivations), beyond the text (what if?), and about the text (regarding comparisons to other books) and to realize that there are questions that lead to discovery and questions that only lead to distraction

Lesson

Model how readers think of questions and hold on to them while reading a story. Demonstrate the difference between questions that lead to further discovery and questions that may distract.

Student Extension

The teacher records questions children raise during read-aloud, and the students collectively sort these into discovery and distracting questions.

Right from the beginning of the year, I model questioning as I read aloud to the class. Fairy tales offer a wonderful opportunity to focus on this strategy in depth. By this time in the year, the children are also more ready to apply this strategy independently with some guidance.

I read *The Little Red Hen* to the class. As I read, I pause at strategic points and ask questions about the characters, actions, and events in the story. Some of my questions are superficial ("Why is the hen called the Little Red Hen?") while others have scope for unpacking the story ("Why does nobody want to help her?" and "Why does she stay with these animals if they are so lazy?").

I write down my questions on sticky notes and put them on an easel next to me, adding any questions the children raise as well. I then explain that when we ask questions that allow us to enter a story while reading it, we are asking discovery questions. However, there are questions that take us into the story and questions that confuse us and lead us away from a better understanding of the story. These are distracting questions.

I divide a chart paper into two columns and title them Discovery Questions and Distracting Questions. I suggest that we put questions that help us understand the story better on one side and the ones that don't on the other. We take up each question, discuss it, and then place it in one of the columns on the chart paper. We repeat this exercise at regular intervals.

This is also a good time to refine working on the question, Does this book remind me of other books I have read or heard before? I choose several books that are spin-offs of popular fairy tales. These include *Once Upon a Golden Apple* by Jean Little, Maggie De Vries, and Phoebe Gilman; *Beware of the Storybook Wolves* by Lauren Child; *The Three Little Wolves and the Big Bad Pig* by Eugene Trivizas; *Help Yourself, Little Red Hen* by Alvin Granowsky; and *Can You See What I See? Once Upon a Time* by Walter Wick.

I read *Once Upon a Golden Apple*. This picture book is about a father making up a fairy tale to tell his two children. While telling his story, he injects humorous, inappropriate phrases in place of more traditional ones. For instance he begins his story, "Once upon a golden apple" instead of "Once upon a time." When his children protest, he modifies this to "Once upon a magic pebble"! Only after he chooses the appropriate phrase do the children let him move on to the next part of his story. My class quickly gets the idea and chimes in with the "no, no, no!" whenever I read the inapt parts. The story brings in several characters, scenes, and dialogues from different fairy tales but merrily mixes them up.

After reading, I tell the children that sometimes when I read, my mind asks me, "Does this book remind me of other books?" I ask them whether the story they just heard reminded them of other books they were familiar with. The references are so vivid that it is very easy for the children to make connections to other stories. Elijah cannot stop chortling as he shares how the princess's comment upon meeting the prince—"Off with his head!"—reminded him of *Alice in Wonderland*, and he doubles over again as, between giggles, he gasps, "That is so silly! She would never say that!" We continue to weave this strategy in as I read the other stories I have selected. I want the children to be completely marinated in story-telling before we begin to write our own fairy tales. ♜

5

THE STORYTELLER'S TALE

What makes a good story? Who is a good storyteller? As I watch a CNN commercial one evening, the sonorous voice of Christiane Amanpour informs me that a "good story is one that captures the essence of its emotions." Another reporter shows up briefly to say, "Every day I have a story to tell." In his book *How to Write Your Life Story*, Ralph Fletcher writes, "A good story should have three basic ingredients: characters (people/pets), setting (place/location) and plot (events/action)" (2007, 3). In my class, Emma tells me, "Paulette [Bourgeois] is a really good storyteller. She writes lots of details." Josiah adds that she makes lots of pictures. From my own literacy training, I know that a good story should have characters we care about encounter challenges that are ultimately resolved. Weaving my training with my real-life connections and my students' evolving understanding of stories and storytelling, I imagine the next few weeks of writing stories.

EXPANDING THE WRITING WORKSHOP

The following lessons expand the writing workshop through a series of focus lessons that once again deliberately mirror the lessons for expanding the reading workshop. We start exploring story planning and story writing in depth after we have worked on deconstructing our favorite stories in reading workshop for a while. After we have a common level of under-standing of how stories work, we are in a position to apply that knowl-edge independently.

FOCUS LESSON | *Stories Have Settings*

Purpose   *To recognize that stories take place in particular settings that have unique characteristics to identify and differentiate them*

Lesson   *Brainstorm a list of settings where stories can take place.*

Student Extension   *Students illustrate and paint life-size representations of different settings.*

As we meet for writing workshop, I ask the children to look around the room and observe the vibrant drawings they've created of their favorite stories. Glued behind and hanging below these pictures are the sheets they've worked on to break up their stories into different parts: beginnings, middles, and ends; characters and settings; and problems and solutions. I refer to all the work we've accomplished so far and tell the children that we are now going to focus on specific parts of stories in more detail. We begin with thinking about places where stories happen, and I ask the children to think about all the stories they know and love and really focus on the setting of these stories. The children and I then brainstorm a list of possible places. The list reflects very diverse settings, such as castles and forests and outer space, and also very specific settings, such as a palace under the sea and a cave in the mountains. I ask the children whether they would like to convert our classroom into a set for stories, and there is much excitement at this thought.

We divide up into teams and over the next few days draw, paint, and construct life-size sceneries that we hang from our ceiling or paint directly onto the bulletin board in our meeting area that will be the set for our future plays. Each morning, the children come in and wonder at the magical transformation of their classroom.

A group of children have decided to add a beanstalk growing up to the ceiling and divide into smaller teams to work on twisting the vines or cutting up leaves that seem to defy all laws of nature! Observing the level of engagement and enthusiasm for their project is a sheer delight.

Another group argues that though we have a castle, we also need a palace. I am unsure of the finer distinctions here but again am ready to follow their lead. We raid our junk building box and hunt for empty cereal boxes, cartons, toilet-paper rolls, glue sticks, and other vital palace-building material. Again I watch as the children work cooperatively, assigning each other tasks and then trying to fit all the pieces together. We finish the palace with coats of paint and an abundance of gold glitter.

The excitement of the children is so contagious that paint-spilled class-rooms and clothes are forgiven by custodians and parents alike. I have cut out doorways in the castle and the cottage, and the children can actually go in and out of these structures. Similarly the forest has spaces between the trees to allow for movement. Parents, siblings, and children from next door linger in our room, caught up in the enchanted landscape. ♜

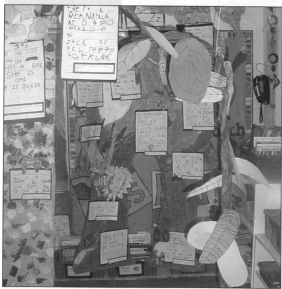

FOCUS LESSON

Stories Have Characters

Purpose   *To understand that stories have characters with unique characteristics that distinguish, differentiate, and identify them*

Lesson   *Brainstorm a list of characters in stories. Discuss how to imagine special characteristics to identify them and then recreate these images.*

Student Extension   *Students choose different story characters to illustrate.*

As with the settings, we next brainstorm a list of story characters. Again the list is very long given the children's familiarity with stories. We then get ready to illustrate these characters. I tell the class that if I were to draw a particular character, I would need to think very hard about what I know about that character. Is the character old or young? Does she or he have any special features? How do I perceive the character? Mean, angry, sad, happy, naughty, good, beautiful, brave, powerful, or scared? How would I try to draw that feature so that someone looking at my picture gets a good idea of the character?

I model drawing a large-scale picture of a character I have chosen, pausing to solicit opinions and suggestions and thinking aloud as I draw. Then I ask the children to choose their characters and draw them, remind-

ing them to think both before they draw and while they are drawing, as I did. We hand out large sheets of watercolor paper and permanent markers and the children draw their characters and then fill them in with watercolors. We then carefully cut out the drawings.

Once the character cutouts are complete, we choose settings from the range of scenery we made earlier on which to display them. The classroom landscape changes yet again to include princesses perched atop our castle, looking over its ramparts and through its windows while knights and soldiers march below. Magical creatures roam the mountains and hills, and the ocean teems with different species of sea creatures, gorgeous in their many hues. The forest is home to beasts and birds—some fierce, some friendly. Girls and boys, moms and dads, brothers and sisters settle into comfortable corners of our cottage. Our storybook land invites us to wander through and let our imaginations explore its possibilities. ♜

FOCUS LESSON *Stories Have a Sense of Time*

Purpose   *To recognize that time is an essential anchor of a story setting because it conveys a sense of when the story takes place*

Lesson   *Model how time can be conveyed through a selection of books that portray time in different ways.*

Student Extension   *Students illustrate stage props that can be used to convey time.*

I have gathered together some familiar books that depict the passage of time very clearly: *When This Box Is Full* by Patricia Lillie (months of the year), *Today Is Monday* by Eric Carle (days of the week), and *The Grouchy Ladybug* by Eric Carle (changes during the course of a day). I show these books to the children and tell them that I have picked them out as a group because they all show time in different ways. I ask them if they can tell what I mean as I briefly skim through the books and then invite comments.

"This book is about January and February and my birthday is in February," "*Today Is Monday* is like our days of the week song but a little bit different," "This one has a clock on each page and the sun looks different" are some of the children's observations.

I tell the children that if I were trying to describe time in my story I could use any of these tricks, like describing what day it is or what month or even what time it is. I have also marked pages in several other books from our classroom library that have phrases such as "Once upon a time," "On a dark and stormy night," "It was a sunny morning," "A long time ago," and "The next day," and I read these relevant sections to the children. I tell them that if I were writing a story, I could use these phrases as well.

We discuss how we could represent time in our play sets and brainstorm ideas. We decide to paint a sun and a moon among clouds to distinguish between night and day and some representations of the seasons to show whether it is summer, fall, winter, or spring. These are interchangeable illustrations that are mounted on meter sticks that can be propped up by stage helpers or the narrator as the story performance unfolds. We divide into teams to draw and paint and mount. The finished paintings are propped up near our performance area to be used as needed. ♟

FOCUS LESSON ## *Stories Have Problems*

Purpose

To create story problems to bring about a story curve

Lesson

Guide a group of students to use a familiar story problem with new story characters.

Student Extension

Students practice storytelling with different characters, using familiar problems but enhancing them with new, sometimes unexpected twists.

I invite the children to draw one of their favorite characters with black permanent markers on overhead transparencies and offer fabric color markers to color in details. We then cut these out. I remind the children of the discussion we had about story problems during our reading workshop—how there may be many little problems but usually just one central problem; how sometimes problems occur in threes; how problems help make the story more interesting to the reader; and how problems are usually solved by the end of the story. I tell them that sometimes these problems can be very simple.

I show them Eric Carle's book *The Grouchy Ladybug* and ask the kids what the central problem is in the story. "He was grouchy and didn't want to be anybody's friend" is the general consensus. I ask whether they can try telling a similar story with a similar problem with their characters and choose four volunteers. We gather in a semicircle around the projector, and I ask the children to place their characters on the top, one by one, as they tell the story, modeling the problem on the one in *The Grouchy Ladybug*. The overhead projector becomes a stage across which the children's character transparencies move. While the transparencies are not large, the images they throw up onto the screen are huge, vibrantly colored, fabulous, and fantastic. We refer to these transparencies as light puppets, and they become additional props that we store in a basket in our storytelling area.

The use of light puppets is an extension of earlier experiences that the children have had of storytelling with props, which included finger puppets—in itself an extension of finger plays popular in most kindergarten rooms. The transition from chanting "Where is ring man?" to retelling *Goldilocks* through finger puppets to recreating a familiar story with unique character light puppets seems seamless. The reason is that the children have been immersed in the experience and have had many opportunities to practice this. Now, only the materials have changed and once the children understand how to use them, they are ready to stretch the bounds of their previous experience by exploring something that is only a little bit new and unfamiliar.

The first story that unfolds has a grouchy mouse who has no friends. The grouchy mouse shouts, "Hey, you want to fight?" to a host of other characters—a butterfly, a teddy bear, a dog, a girl, and a lion. Each character responds to this taunt by replying, "If you insist." The mouse does not stay to fight but scurries away till he finds someone else. By the end, he is tired and has given up the idea of fighting.

As one group finishes, another one takes over. We raid our library to find different stories from which we may borrow a problem to enact with our very own characters. I keep a supply of transparency paper and pens, and the children continue to make more drawings to use over the next few days. They begin to include settings in their drawings, and I remind them that they can also include details to show what time of day or season it is as they draw. ♜

FOCUS LESSON — *Stories Have Solutions to Problems*

Purpose — To create solutions to their stories within the story itself

Lesson — Choose six students to create and enact an original story. Children sit in a circle and choose to enact certain story characters. The first two children start the story, the third and fourth include a problem, and the last two think of a solution. Once the story is done, the group is ready to perform.

Student Extension — Students create and enact their own stories independently.

We come to this point after we've spent some time acting out familiar stories in our performance area and playing with our light puppets on the overhead projector. I tell the children that as readers, they are now very familiar with retelling and enacting familiar stories as well as creating slight twists on their favorite stories with their light puppets. I ask them whether they would like to think as writers now and create their own stories with their own problems and then perform those stories. I invite six volunteers to help with the first creation and enactment. By now the class is adept at dividing itself up into performers and audience, and the transition is very quick. I ask the children to watch what I do with the volunteers and then they can do this on their own.

I ask my volunteers to choose the characters they would like to have in their story. The children look around at the illustrated characters pinned up around our sets and choose for themselves. We sit in a circle. I tell the children that we are going to create our own story, but we have to be sure to include all the characters and to have a problem that can be solved by one or more of the characters. We start off our discussion in a clockwise direction with each child adding on a line to the story. I ask the first two children to start the story. When we get to the third and fourth person, I ask them to include a problem, and it's then up to the last two to think of a solution. Once our story is done, we are ready to perform.

We continue to perform our own stories regularly. There are days that the performing group functions smoothly with minimal intervention; on other days, specific group dynamics play out differently and require my attention. Such events prompt further discussion and help make the necessity of different story elements clearer.

One day Elijah, who has chosen to play a king, flounces out of the play area, protesting that he doesn't like the story problem that his partners have created. When asked, the group tells me that in their story the king loses his powers. A mouse helps restore it with the help of the girl who cleans the castle. I ask the group whether they followed our model established to create stories and they affirm that they did do so. Elijah is still unhappy at playing a powerless king, and he is adamant in his refusal to do so. "But then our story won't work!" exclaims Josiah. I suggest to Elijah that he can either switch his role with someone else this time or create a different version of the story the next time but that it would be really unfair to leave his friends without his support. The group is keen to see this resolved so that they can perform for their audience, and we finally reach a compromise.

Each time we face a problem and have to effect a compromise or resolution, the part that each character plays in a story is made clearer in the ensuing discussion, as is the fact that no part in a story is minor or unimportant—they all fit together for a reason. ♖

Writing Descriptions of Settings

Purpose   To recognize that giving voice to imagination paves the way for adding details to descriptions and makes a setting come alive for a reader

Lesson   Model writing a description for a particular place, describing not just its external appearance but also your imaginings about it.

Student Extension   Students choose a place from the previously made list of places where stories happen and write descriptions.

As we built our play sets or drew out our characters, I encouraged the children to talk as they worked. When we put words to our imaginings, I told them, we start noticing and putting in more details. The children are growing increasingly adept at articulating their imagined pictures and executing these onto a canvas. I know all this talk will help us when we actually put pen to paper to write descriptions of people and places.

I gather the children in front of my writing easel and tell them that we are going to write descriptions of our settings. We go over our list of places where stories happen, and I choose to write about a castle. As I write, I tell the children that the first thing I am going to be thinking about is what the castle looks like. I look over at the castle in our classroom and briefly write a minimal description: "The castle is big."

"Does this give you all the information about the castle, or do you wish that I had written more?" I ask. "You need to write more or it will be boring to read," asserts Min Jae. Thanking Min Jae for her observation, I explain that today I will share a trick with them. "Sometimes when I write about a place, I don't just write about what I can see on the outside. I also imagine what could be possible inside that place. Does the place have some magic? Do special people live there? Do strange and wonderful things happen there? What do I feel about this place? What do others think about this place?" I explain that when I include all or some of these answers in my description, I make the place more real for the person reading my writing. I complete my description of the castle with much shared input from the children.

I invite them to pick out places from our list that they would like to describe, and once they've finished, we pin these descriptions onto the scenes around our classroom. ♜

FOCUS LESSON

Writing Character Descriptions and Dialogue

Purpose
To learn how to write detailed descriptions of a character that helps make that character real in the reader's mind

Lesson
Model writing a description of a character, thinking of what the character is like externally as well as internally.

Student Extension
Students choose a character from the previously created list of characters who are found in stories and write descriptions.

Our class Big Book *The Enormous Watermelon*, with illustrations of fairy-tale characters and matching dialogue written by the children, is very popular. We read the book, and I remind the children that different characters speak and behave differently. I ask them whether they remember how we wrote descriptions of the scenes around our room and say that we can describe characters in a similar way by focusing not just on the outside but also on the inside—how the character thinks, feels, or acts. We can also include dialogue as a way to do this.

I model writing a character description, including some dialogue, and then pass out the character illustrations the children did earlier and ask them to write descriptions. As they write, I encourage them to add details to their writing.

Elijah has made a dinosaur, and he writes, "My T-Rex can kill lots of people and scare people. He can fly fast. He has sharp teeth. He has paws. He lands with a thump because he is heavy." Ido's superhero "can fly and run very fast. He eats so much." Describing her dolphin, Emma writes, "The dolphin can swim underwater. His name is Tom. He is weak. When he goes down he really dies."

Roy is diligently writing about a unicorn but I see no illustration before him. "What happened to your picture, Roy?" I ask. "Don't you know my unicorn is invisible—so how can I draw him?" replies Roy, very logically. Unfortunately, his logic cannot hide the fact that I know that he dislikes drawing and seeks any excuse to wriggle out of it! I also know that one of the reasons Roy doesn't like drawing is that his imagination is way beyond his actual motor skills with pen and paper. As a writer, Roy needs the practice that drawing detailed pictures will give him for reasons more basic than coaxing the words out of his imagination. I ask Roy to choose another character that he can draw after he has finished with his unicorn, and he agrees as he sees his friends move on to other characters once their originals are completed. Once all the character descriptions are finished, I put them up alongside the character illustrations hanging on the scenes around our room. ♜

FOCUS LESSON *Writing Golden Lines*

Purpose
To become familiar with common phrases that can be used to start and end stories

Lesson
Write out common phrases from fairy tales—story starters, story endings, descriptions of settings, descriptions of actions, and commonly used dramatic expressions—onto separate pieces of card stock. Sort them into categories with the students and display them around the room.

Student Extension
Students use these phrases when they enact their stories and later when they write their stories.

Phrases that have become immortalized in literature because of their popular usage are referred to as golden lines in our class. I have written out several such evocative phrases from popular fairy tales on separate pieces of card stock. These phrases include story starters such as "Once upon a time," "A long time ago," "On a dark and stormy night"; descriptions of places such as "In a land far, far away," "In a castle above the clouds," "Deep below the sea"; descriptions of actions such as "And he huffed and he puffed," "He climbed and he climbed," "And she did!"; sound words such as *Poof!, Abracadabra, Ouch!, Boom!*; and story endings such as "They lived happily ever after," "They found a pot of gold at the end of the rainbow," "They sailed away into the sunset."

I read out each phrase and tell the children that these are lines that writers often use when they write fairy tales. I ask them if they can help me sort these into categories. Which phrases could we use to start a story or to end it? Which phrases would describe places or actions and which are expressions that we could use to add drama to our story? After the discussion and sorting, I tell the children that these pieces of card stock are going to hang around our classroom and they are welcome to use the phrases as they create their own stories. ♜

Exploring Story Planning

Purpose

To plan the distinct parts of a story before writing and to understand that the story unfolds from the interactions of different characters within particular settings

Lesson

Model planning an original story using Parts of a Story 1 and 2.

Student Extension

Students plan their own stories.

Now we are ready to write our own stories. The ground is fertile for this endeavor, as the children have been immersed in reading and retelling popular fairy tales and in creating and performing their own.

There is a palpable sense of excitement in the class. I had told the children that today we were going to start writing our very own fairy tales. We gather on the rug and quickly go over our What Do Good Writers Do? anchor chart as a group. I add the list of new strategies that we have been working on since we began exploring fairy tales to this chart, and we go over these too.

I ask the children what we would need to include in our story to make it interesting to the reader. "Characters, we need good guys and bad guys," says Elijah. I reinforce Elijah's point by reminding the children of the times we tried to act out stories where all the characters were similar and behaved in exactly the same manner and how dull these stories were for the audience because there was no tension or excitement. "We need to have places for them to live" is another comment that tags onto the last discussion. "We should have a problem and some magic," says Roy, who is still determined to write about his invisible unicorn. Jasmine, who has absolutely adored playacting and making up dialogues, tells us that she wants to make her characters say things to each other.

I pass out blank Parts of a Story 1 sheets and model how I can use the sheets to plan my story. I muse about the characters I may wish to write about and deliberate about my choices. I emphasize that I would like to limit my cast of characters to three or four to better control the story. As I choose characters to write about and briefly sketch them, I start talking about their personalities. What are these characters like inside? Are they happy or sad? Do they have some special wishes or are they in the midst of some problem? I then look through the choices of settings before me and decide on a couple of places to set my story. The characters are going to move between these places, and maybe this will impact the way the story flows. I also think about a time to frame my story. Is it morning or evening? Winter or summer? I ask the children to use their own sheets to plan their stories.

I follow this lesson with another one on thinking about the main problem of my story and its solution. I pass out blank Parts of a Story 2 sheets and decide on what the central problem could be in my story. How is this problem going to be resolved? ♜

FOCUS LESSON | *Exploring Story Writing*

Purpose　*To reinforce all that we've learned about story structure in previous lessons by writing our own stories*

Lesson　*Paper clip three sets of papers, each set containing a blank page and a lined page. Model using these to illustrate and write the beginning, middle, and end of a story.*

Student Extension　*Students illustrate and write their own stories, working on one set at a time.*

I ask the children whether they are going to tell their entire story in one page, and there is a chorus of dissent. I take a sheet of blank paper and one of lined paper and paper clip them together. I make three such sets and then tell the children that each set is for a specific part of my story, the beginning, the middle, or the end. However, I may want to change around the story as I get more ideas and that is why I am not ready to staple it all together right now. I tell the children that I am going to work on one part of my story at a time—starting at the beginning—so that I can put all the details I need into my illustration and writing. I remind the children that once they come to the second set, they need to start thinking about a problem and writing about it. They have to solve the problem by the third set so that they can end their story. "And then we write 'They lived happily ever after' at the end!" exclaims Kayleigh. "And we have to write 'Once upon a time' in the beginning," chimes in Josiah, who loves having the final word on any subject. With Josiah's comment spurring us on, I ask the children to move to their writing spots so that they can start work on their own fairy tales.

We earlier decided to illustrate our stories in Eric Carle's style. We studied his artwork in great detail when he was our author of the month and made a lot of paper in his instantly recognizable, brightly patterned, vivid colors. We also studied how he collages his illustrations. Now we are going to blend our knowledge of the artist's style to our study of fairy tales and create something unique of our own.

We work on our stories for a couple of weeks, illustrating, writing, and refining as I walk around and conference as needed. The children regularly share their work from the Author's Chair.

The children's writing displays the diverse abilities and personalities in our classroom. Jasmine's and Josiah's stories are extremely well developed. Jasmine's story has a unique cast of characters that includes an "animal girl," a saber-tooth tiger, and a swan. She crafts a central problem that is resolved within the story. Jasmine uses elegant story language, such as "Once upon a time" to open her story and "They lived happily ever after" to close it.

Jasmine's story: *"Once upon a time there was an animal girl and a saber tooth and they were in the forest and there was magical grass."*

"And then the animal girl and the saber tooth got lost in the forest and they screamed help and the swan heard them and the swan got closer and closer."

ε

And the son
Brot them to
Hom And
they sed them
you The y sed
the End And they
livd HaPly evr
AFtr

"And the swan brought them home and they said, 'Thank you' and they said, 'The end' and they lived happily ever after."

She also experiments with using dialogue. Her illustrations carry her story forward and give the reader a clear picture of the scenes she has visualized in her imagination. Josiah's story is of a similar quality. He carries his visualizations a step further into actual written descriptions of the central characters as well as the setting of his story. Josiah is one of the few children in the classroom who experiments with rising action. He uses the formula of events happening in threes to propel his story forward. His illustrations, however, are fairly basic.

An illustration from Josiah's story

Some other children are working at refining their storytelling skills. While they demonstrate their engagement with the lessons taught, they are in the process of further developing their expertise through teacher intervention. Kayleigh's immersion in fairy tales is clear from the way she describes her main character—the "very slow turtle." She uses this description as a refrain to establish a pattern in her story. Her story is elegantly sequenced, and there is a clear sense of hero and villain. Kayleigh's illustrations depict the central idea in each sequence but are not very well developed. Min Jae writes about three friends—a rabbit, a princess, and a squirrel. She has a clear story problem that reflects her real-life experience with her friends. Min Jae's illustrations are very finely detailed and exact, inviting the reader into her story world. She paces her story into a clear beginning, middle, and end and works hard to invoke drama and tension.

Min Jae's story: "Once upon a time there was a rabbit and a princess and a squirrel. They were playing hide-and-seek and the squirrel was looking for the rabbit and the princess. Then the squirrel went to hide. It was a sunny day."

and tay cum to the
Hoose but tar
was no scwrs. And
tay fnod, ond tay
fnoD but tar.
Wos no Scwrs. And
it caM a evning.

"The rabbit and the princess came to the house but there was no squirrel. They looked and they looked but there was no squirrel. It became evening."

day foon the scwurs
byhind the tree. and
the. prinSas. and
a rabit wus
hpi a'boot scwr̥s
And it kaM
hit and tai
PLaihpLievra̶tt.

"They found the squirrel behind a tree and the princess and the rabbit were happy about the squirrel. It became night and they were playing happily ever after."

A few children have marvelous story ideas but need significant help in executing them. Roy's story problem is extremely distinctive—a friend who is invisible. He uses beautiful story language imbued with his inimitable flair for adding drama to his story. Roy's storytelling abilities, however, far outpace his motor abilities, and his illustrations are extremely minimal. Brian's story also has a distinctive central problem—a unicorn who loses his magic when it is cloudy and regains it when it is sunny. Brian creates a special character who helps resolve the problem for the unicorn.

Although Brian employs story structure to craft his story, his pacing is a little abrupt as the problem is resolved very suddenly. ♜

Brian's story

the rooNUcooRN
AND THE RABFt
AND THEBUPRf
LI WR FRØ
NS tHEA
LIVD IN
THE FOORTst

"*The unicorn and the rabbit and the butterfly were friends and they lived in the forest.*"

WONDAWAN
HIt WUS
CLOOtE
tHEtOONICOO
LOOStHIsMAGIC
BUt WANHIt
WUSSUN E
HEGOtHIS
MAOF
BAC

"*When it was cloudy the unicorn lost his magic but when it was sunny he got his magic back.*"

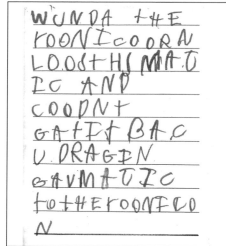

"One day the unicorn lost his magic and he couldn't get it back. The dragon gave magic to the unicorn."

| FOCUS LESSON | *Writing Story Titles* |

| Purpose | To choose a title with deliberation and careful thought and convey through that title the image the writer wants to project |

| Lesson | Choose books that represent different categories of titles—titles that name the main character, identify the main problem, and give the main idea. Discuss how these categories are different, and then sort the books with the students. |

| Student Extension | Students write titles for their own stories. |

I have been illustrating and writing my own story as a model for the class at the beginning of our writing workshop every day. My story is now ready as are those of many of the children. I have picked out several popular fairy tales along with many of our favorite read-alouds from our classroom library, and I tell the children that today we are going to focus on writing story titles.

Naming a story is a moment of great significance for an author. I ask the children to recall what they learned about writing titles while writing personal narratives. I tell them that writing titles for fiction can follow similar patterns. Sometimes titles can be very straightforward and simple and just name the characters in the story like *The Little Red Hen* by

Lucinda McQueen. Sometimes the titles can talk about the big problem in the story like *Rainbow Fish to the Rescue* by Marcus Pfister. And sometimes titles could give the main idea of the story like *Will You Be My Friend? A Bunny and Bird Story* by Nancy Tafuri. We sit in a circle, and I place the books I have talked about in the middle. I pass out the other books I have collected around the circle and invite the children to notice the title of the book they have received and place it in an appropriate pile in the middle.

I deliberately keep the categories very basic and limited at this stage so that it is something the children can very easily understand and apply on their own. After our discussion and sorting, I ask the children to think about what kind of title they might write for their story and to move to their writing spots once they have an idea. ♜

TIME TO CELEBRATE

I gather the children together and explain that we are now going to be publishing more grown-up versions of their stories, books that look like real-life books. "Then we can put them in the library for everyone to read!" exclaims Elijah. I see Jasmine looking a little disturbed at this and ask what is bothering her. "I don't want my book to go far away to someone's house, and it will, if someone borrows it from the library," wails Jasmine. I appreciate the feelings that these different statements express—a pride in one's work as well as a sense of ownership and possessiveness—and I know we have come a long way in seeing ourselves as readers and writers. We reach a compromise by agreeing to display these books in our classroom library and putting up a poster in the school library that invites readers to come and discover new and exciting authors in our kindergarten room. But first we have to get the books ready.

I explain to the children that after writing their stories, authors collaborate with their editors before publishing their books. The editor's job, I clarify, is to make sure that all the words of the author can be read and understood by the reader. "But that's what you do. Is a teacher an editor?" asks Josiah. I reply that in classrooms, teachers do moonlight as editors and I'd be happy to be theirs! The fantasy of being an author is real and palpable for these children—they absolutely believe they have written stories that can be read and enjoyed by everybody, and there is no self-consciousness or inhibition about their work. This persona is as easily donned as that of an architect of marvelous constructions, a chef of culinary marvels, or an artist of great achievement—the children's play is their work, and they invest it with energy, enthusiasm, and life force. I have tried to channel this life force toward achieving ambitious goals, but because the medium has remained playful and pretend, there has been a seamless extension of their personalities as architects and chefs and artists to include those of readers and writers. They also believe that as real authors, they need real editors! I am happy to sustain this belief and enact the role of an editor over the next few days. I sit with individual children at my computer and type out their stories. We make changes as necessary. We put the typed pages together with their illustrations, add the title page, and bind the books. I staple their original handwritten pages as well.

For each child, I place his or her bound book on one side of a two-pocket paper folder. On the other side, I place the handwritten draft. We glue the cover page to the front of the folder, and we display the finished folders in our classroom library. We are now ready to celebrate with an authors' party. Unlike last trimester's private party, limited to just our class, this time we will invite our parents and families, other teachers, and administrators. I also usually try to time this trimester's authors' party with the tour of a visiting author and invite him or her as well.

This year, Johanna Hurwitz and Mordicai Gerstein are visiting the school. Both authors are delighted at the idea of meeting kindergarten authors. When we finally meet Johanna, my kids are prepared with a list of questions they have thought of to ask a real author. Jasmine asks, "Do you always write stories from real life?" Johanna tells us how a lot of her stories are based on her life, and we get a glimpse into the real life of an author. Elijah asks, "Do you always think first?" and Brian wants to know whether she writes every day and how many books she makes a day! Josiah asks, "Do you have an editor?" and then kindly clarifies that an "editor is like a teacher but more grown-up"! Johanna is amazed at these questions that exhibit an emerging understanding of the reading and writing process. "Are these kindergartners?" she asks me. With a lump in my throat, I nod. I am so proud at the connections these little people have made and how articulate they are in expressing themselves. There is no hesitation as they talk to Johanna; she is after all a fellow author just like them even though one of her answers is a little disappointing. Johanna tells us that while she writes every day, her books take months to get ready. "Huh!" says Roy. "*We* make books every day!"

Mordicai is equally delighted to meet his fellow authors. The children line up to share their books with him, and he patiently listens to each child read his or her story, compliments their work, and encourages them to keep on writing. The children leave this meeting with gilded auras around them, walking ten feet tall!

With their folders in front of them, the children await the arrival of the rest of our invited guests. There is a great sense of anticipation and much delight. However, I observe that their author personas are very much in place today—a certain stature and maturity that comes from accomplishment. Right on time, our guests arrive. The parents naturally gravitate toward their own children first, but I have asked them to circulate around and read the books of other students as well. The idea is that the audience will come to the author, who will remain seated in his or her chosen spot.

Within minutes, everybody is reading in the room. People are arranged in groups around tables, on the rugs, in and around our play sets—in the castle, behind the forest, perched on the mountain, or wading in the ocean. I stand back and direct traffic, take photographs, and write quick anecdotal notes. I notice that most children want to share their handwritten drafts once the books have been seen—it is perhaps more real to them. Their conversation is peppered with the terms that we have been using this trimester, demonstrating their familiarity with the genre studied and an ease with deconstructing and recreating it. With a deep sense of satisfaction, I know that we have achieved what we had imagined at the beginning of this exploration: we have expanded the reading and writing workshop and are now ready for the next stage, to further extend this process in the last and final trimester of the kindergarten year.

6

THE REVIEWS
ARE IN

Each New Year I make a resolution to lose weight. I chart out an ambitious weight-loss program and resolve to follow it with zealous effort. I make myself an elaborate weight-loss planner. I dream of the wonderful new wardrobe I will treat myself to upon my success. I count calories and exercise. And usually by about mid-March, my resolution is in shambles, the planner stashed away in some hidden corner, the unwanted pounds as ensconced as ever!

The only year I succeeded in not only losing the undesired pounds but also keeping them off was the year I kept a diary. This was no fancy diary but my regular daily diary. I just made some additions to it. On the first page, I recorded my current weight and my dream weight. Then I wrote down my plan. I decided to follow my usual weight-loss regimen, but this time, I would check in daily and record whether I had followed my exercise and diet plan or not. I would also weigh myself weekly and record that in my diary.

During the initial weeks, my diary recorded minimal changes, but after a month, I could see a significant loss. Bolstered by my success, I persevered and eventually achieved my target weight—and shopped around for a well-deserved new wardrobe! To this day, I think that what engineered my success was the reality of the weekly weigh-ins against the vision of a result.

Even though the contexts are vastly different, I think that student success is ensured by a similar application of long-term learning goals, tempered with regular check-ins. Anyone who has taught a class of five- and six-year-olds knows the reality and the challenge of managing that class. Assessment therefore needs to be embedded in instruction as a continuous and ongoing process. It has to be conceived and executed within the context of daily instruction. To conceive it as an added layer is to make the process exhausting, unmanageable, and ultimately unsuccessful. Maintaining records of this process also has to be streamlined, effective, and accessible—maybe refining something that is already in current use rather than creating an elaborate superstructure imposed on the existing system.

Three essential questions guide me as I plan my assessment portfolio every year:

1. What do I want my students to know and be able to do?
2. How will I know they know this and are able to do this?
3. How will I check in to see that they are in the process of gaining this knowledge or skill?

The first question is addressed through envisioning a yearlong curriculum and identifying specific learning targets that support reading and writing. The second question is addressed by identifying and evaluating individual student samples that show evidence of the projected learning targets. The last question is addressed through ongoing formative assessment that takes the form of individual assessments, anecdotal records, and conference notes. Instruction, evaluation, and assessment are inextricably interlinked and dependent on one another.

MATCHING INSTRUCTION TO ASSESSMENT

The yearlong literacy overview is the starting point for planning my instruction every year. I review each trimester block and the learning envisaged in that time in the areas of reading, writing, and word study. I consciously plan and use natural connections within these subject areas. There is also a goal for each subject in that particular trimester. This goal is broken up into specific scaffolded learning targets. The learning targets are highlighted during reading workshop through shared reading, interactive read-alouds, and independent reading. The writing targets are the instructional emphasis during writing workshop through shared writing, interactive writing, and independent writing. The word-study lessons are an opportunity to use, practice, and refine many of the skills used in reading and writing. The context for these lessons is shared reading and literacy stations.

Before embarking on the focus lessons, I assess my students individually so that I am able to differentiate as necessary. This is imperative, as the children are all at varying levels of skill, understanding, and ability. I mold my instruction according to the levels I perceive, which may be different from year to year.

During the period of immersion in daily instruction, I continually check in with my students by maintaining anecdotal records and through informal conferences. I try to assess what I have taught. These check-ins enable me to give my instruction new direction if necessary. If I stuck only to my overview, my teaching would become top heavy and not in touch with the reality of my students' needs. If I taught only in response, my teaching would become rudderless, without any standards of achievement or excellence. I rely on my anecdotal and conference notes to keep in touch with what my students need, and I rely on my overview to move them in the direction I want them to go.

PUTTING THE PIECES TOGETHER

There are four essential pieces that make up my assessment portfolio. These are *individual student folders, a reading conference folder, a writing conference folder*, and *student portfolios*. Each is constituted slightly differently, but they all contribute to one another and to overall evaluation.

Individual Student Folders

Each student in our class has an assessment folder. On one side of this two-pocket folder, I keep photocopies of all the individual literacy assessments that are required during the course of the year. These include forms to assess concepts of print (adapted from Marie Clay) and forms to assess the recognition of letters, sounds and words, beginning and end phonemes, rhyming words, and chunks within words. In the beginning of the year, I interview each child about his or her reading, and this record is also stored within this folder (see Appendix for a blank reading survey form). I also have a form on which the children write their names and draw their self-portraits at different times over the course of the year (see

Reading Survey   Jasmine
                                        Aug '05

	Yes	No
Do you like reading?	Yes	No
Are you a good reader?	Yes	No
Do you have favourite books?	Yes	No
Do you like to talk about books?	Yes	No
Do you like to tell stories?	Yes	No

Where are you reading? On my bed - I mean at the hotel's bed!

Who is reading with you? By myself.

What are you reading? A princess book. Cinderella. I really like books about animals.

Draw a picture of you reading at home.

Sample reading survey

Appendix for a blank self-portrait form). Besides this, I keep a record of how the children write simple words over the three trimesters. I use this record to check how the students are using beginning and ending sounds and whether they are trying to write middle sounds as well.

Reading Conference Folders

In addition to these individual student folders, I also create a reading conference folder for myself. The reading conference folder is again a two-pocket folder and includes a conference record for each student and a bunch of easy readers at a range of reading levels.

Conference record form

Conference Notes Jasmine

Rainbow Fish 13/9
Ev the big
- Choice ? B'cor the
Rb fish td. a new frd.
- Abt ? RB ev other
fish thght he was
going to eat them
but he was lkg.
at his shiny scales.
- Fav. part ? I don't
know b'cor I haven't

Lkd. at the whole bk
- Wds. ? ✓
- Letters ? ✓
- /f/ sound ? I don't
know

*Jasmine : - This pic.
reminds me of my
garden and the girl on
this page is feeling
happy.

Conference Notes **Jasmine**

I Paint 16/11
- giraffe Christmas tree
- spots, zigzag
- How? "B'coz I lkd at the begg sd"
- ? "And the pics"
- /spots/ If giraffe, what? /g/ ☺
* Stretch out /recheck

Dancing Shoes. 1/12
- TP - Are these...
- Picked up pattern
- rdg. ī expression
- Abt.? A ballerina not knowg what her dancg. shoes are.
- Why I picked it for you? B'coz I like ballet. ↓

I Paint — Jasmine
I reminds me of Painting a giraffe and I could read the whole book. (I Paint snake, I Paint spots) the beginning sound.

Mrs. W.W's Tub. 25/1
- ___ TP: Can you sound it out?
  soap   TP: Lk. at pic.
- Like? Yeah. Why? B'coz it's diffn't fr. the other one & I like all the animals.
- Diffn't? The woods fr the animals lk really funny.

Rumpelstiltskin 7/2
Jan. I saw a king ī his castle

Once Upon...
- Goldilocks fr the 3 bears.
- Snowwhite fr the 7 dwarves

The hungry kitten 28/2
- Smart? I lkd. at the pics. b'coz they give us ans & I lkd at wds & matched up ō pics.

Gingerbread Boy
Jasmine:—
It reminds me of when I saw a real fox like the same in story and

Wood and Paper.
When we were lkg. at wood
Pics are real

I photocopy the yearlong reading overview and glue it onto the front of the folder. I photocopy the yearlong reading focus lessons and glue them onto the back cover. These are to prompt and direct the questions I ask of my students during informal reading conferences. I keep the conference records of all the students in alphabetical order on one side of the folder. For reading conferences, I seek students out to work with them individually. As I confer with each child, I move his or her conference record form (see Appendix for a blank version) from one side of the folder to the other. This way, I go through my whole class and write notes about each child, avoiding the danger of having too many notes on one child and none on another. After I finish conferring with the whole class, I replace all the sheets on the original side and go through the process again.

Writing Conference Folders

The writing conference folder is also a two-pocket folder; inside, there are conference records for each student. However, these records are not alphabetized by name but are grouped according to individual table groups. I also have some samples of my personal writing and student writing that match the focus lessons that I can use as examples. Again, I photocopy the yearlong writing overview and glue it to the front of the folder and photocopy the yearlong writing focus lessons and glue them to the back to guide my writing conferences. I use the writing conference folder in a similar way as I use the reading conference folder, writing notes about individual students in a table group and moving them from one pocket to the other before working with another table group.

For years, I struggled with writing conferences with kindergartners. Coaching a beginning writer through the writing process was exhausting enough without trying to write conference notes at the same time. Eventually, I realized that I was trying to maintain my writing conference notes in much the same way as my reading conference notes when the contexts for the two were vastly different. Reading behavior is ephemeral and intangible. Most of it takes place within the student's mind. If I didn't ask pertinent questions allowing the students to articulate their thoughts and record their responses, the behavior was impossible to reconstitute or understand. Writing, however, left its own tangible record—the actual work done by the student that could be used as a sample later. I realized that I could support the student during our conference, actively coaching and supporting the writing process; jot down minimal notes about the nature of the writing; and then go back after the conference to the student sample and complete my notes. This realization paved the way for far more relaxed and meaningful writing conferences than before.

Student Portfolios

The fourth and final piece in my assessment portfolio is individual student portfolios. These are trifolds made out of card stock with pockets on one side. Each fold represents one trimester. On the side with the pockets, I keep one or two representative examples of writing from each trimester, along with my writing conference notes.

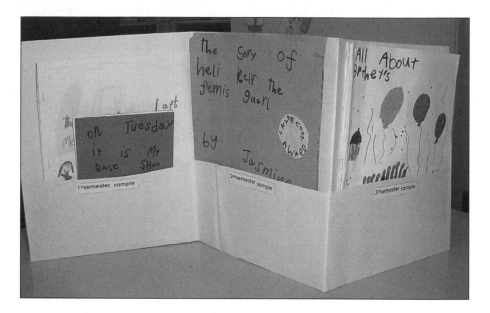

On the other side, I photocopy a page from a just-right book that the student is reading independently and paste it in the proper trimester section. I also save all the reading conference notes from that trimester and staple these in as well.

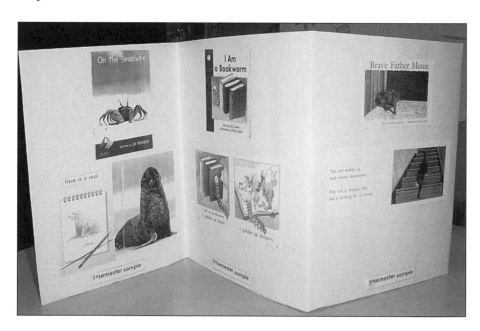

MANAGING THE ASSESSMENT PIECES

I establish procedures for ongoing classroom-based assessment from the beginning of the year. I want assessment to be a natural expectation in our classroom and part of our daily schedule. I want to be able to undertake this within our classroom, amidst my students, with some clear guidelines about how the rest of the class functions during this time.

Right at the beginning of the year, while I'm explaining the daily schedule to my students, I tell them that there will be times when I will need to work with each of them individually. During these times, I will most probably be having a conversation with them and asking them some questions. They may see me taking notes as they talk, as I am very interested in everything they have to say. At other times, I may ask them to do something specific. These times, I stress, are very, very important to me and to the individual student concerned. These times are not to be disturbed by any other student. As a class, we draw up a few simple guidelines about options to explore if the children are stuck, confused, or do not know what to do during this time and need help. I write these up on a chart, illustrate them with simple icons, and hang the chart in our room.

We follow our daily schedule of reading and writing workshops and literacy stations from the first few weeks of the school year. During this time, I try to schedule my reading conferences during the short independent reading block. As the children sit in preferred places around the room, I move around with my reading conference folder, resolutely carrying out hushed conversations with an individual student even though there may be many attempts to gain my attention from another. If the attempt verges toward disruption, I silently point the child toward the options chart, without further engagement. The first few weeks of this process can be excruciatingly frustrating but gradually, as the children become more familiar with their environment and the schedule, this becomes easier. As the length of independent reading time increases, so does my time for individual conferences. I even begin to use this time to carry out individual assessments and later, running records. Following independent reading, we gather together for a share. We sit in a circle, and the children bring books in which they've discovered something they wish to share with their peers. I find this an invaluable time to write anecdotal notes about the children who participate. I write on sticky notes and later paste these into their conference records.

The first few weeks of writing workshop, I try to maintain a semblance of the same conference procedure as during independent reading.

During writing workshop, the children are seated at assigned writing tables. Before I begin work with a particular group, I briefly touch base with all the other tables through short table conferences. I move around to each table, watch the children work for a while, and commend them about something I notice them doing well. I may also take the opportunity to notice a strategy that many at the table could benefit from and coach the group on this particular strategy, keeping it very short and focused. I then move to the table I plan to actually work with and pull out the conference records of all the students in that group. I confer with each child, taking brief notes. As the year gets under way, and the students begin to use the writing-process chart, they can sign up for conferences if they feel the need to do so. In this case, I go directly to those students as I begin my conferences. Independent writing is followed by Author's Chair. Students can sign up if they have some writing to share. Again this time is ideal for writing anecdotal notes about writing behavior.

Since my instructional plan is divided into three trimesters, my assessment plan is similarly distributed. The overarching essential questions ingrained in the literacy overview are broken up into specific learning targets, and it is these that guide my conference questions. (See Appendix for a list of first- and second-semester conference questions.) I keep my conferences very simple, not looking for evidence of many kinds of skills and behaviors at the same time. Rather, I channel my questions around the particular focus lessons I have been teaching. Similarly, I do not plan a barrage of individual assessments simultaneously; I assess the children as I teach a particular skill over the course of the three trimesters.

Beginning of the Year

We begin the year by exploring the reading workshop. Our essential questions are: What are books? What are readers? Who reads? Where do we read? What do we read? How do readers get the message?

LEARNING TARGETS FOR BUILDING READING HABITS	CONFERENCE QUESTIONS/ ANECDOTAL NOTES	ONGOING FORMATIVE ASSESSMENT
Readers form opinions and talk about books.	Why did you choose this book? Do you like/not like the story? Why? Do you have a favorite part?	Reading Survey
Readers make connections as they read.	Does this remind you of something • In your life? • In another book? • In the world around you?	
Readers choose books carefully.	How did you choose this book? Did you • Look at the cover? • Look at the title? • Look at the pictures? • Look at the words? • Choose a book you've heard before?	
Readers value books and their reading time.	How are you reading this book? Are you • Starting from the first page? • Turning the pages one by one? • Using a library voice? • Using the library correctly? • Practicing partner reading?	Concepts of Print
Readers use many strategies to read.	What strategy are you using to read? Are you • Looking at the pictures? • Looking at the words? • Stretching words out like a rubber band and sounding them out? Can you show me how you are reading? Are there some words you can recognize?	Recognition of letters—upper and lower case Recognition of letter sounds Recognition of beginning sounds in words Recognition of end sounds in words Recognition of quick-and-easy words

Similar to reading workshop, we begin the school year by exploring the writing workshop. Our essential questions are: What is writing? Where do we find writing? Who writes? Why do writers write? How do we write?

LEARNING TARGETS FOR DEVELOPING WRITING HABITS	CONFERENCE QUESTIONS/ ANECDOTAL NOTES	ONGOING FORMATIVE ASSESSMENT
Writers draw pictures.	What is your drawing about? Can you show me some details you've added to make your drawing look real?	
Writers think of ideas.	What are you writing about? How did you know what to write?	
Writers tell stories.	What is your story about? What is happening in your story?	
Writers write words.	What strategy are you using to write the words to your story? Are you • Sounding words out? • Writing quick-and-easy words? • Writing words you recognize? • Writing words from dictionaries? • Writing words the best you can? Can you reread your writing?	
Writers write for different purposes.		Student examples of letters, signs, labels
Writers add details to their writing.	Can you tell me the story over your fingers? Have you written the outside and inside of your story?	
Writers send their stories out into the world.	Anecdotal notes about author behavior, audience behavior, asking questions, making suggestions, making comments	Student examples of published narrative
Writers celebrate as a community.		Student examples of messages to their peers

Assessment in Action:
A Look at Jasmine at the Beginning of the Year

Jasmine bounced into the kindergarten classroom, winning friends with her cheerful and generous nature. She was a motivated and eagerly alive learner, excited to make connections between what she knew and what she was learning as a kindergartner, and it was wonderful to see her joy when she made any such discovery. When interviewed at the beginning of the year about her reading habits, Jasmine confidently asserted that she was a good reader who had favorite books and liked to talk about them. She loved princess books and books about animals and said that she also loved to tell stories. When asked to draw a picture of herself reading at home, Jasmine hesitated a bit before confiding that her family still didn't have a home, as they had just moved to the city and were therefore living at a hotel. I asked whether she was reading at the hotel, and she looked up in surprise, assertively declaring, "Of course I am!" I was left with the subtle impression that my question had indeed been very misguided! Jasmine proceeded to draw a picture of herself sprawled in bed with an open book placed on her chest while her sister sat nearby and worked on the laptop (see drawing on page 116).

On Jasmine's first trimester reading conference record, I recorded her initial reading behaviors. I noticed that she often went back to the books I had read aloud to the class. She exhibited many prereading skills, holding books appropriately, identifying letters and words, and trying to guess words based on her knowledge of beginning sounds. She could retell stories. During one of our conferences, I found her reading *The Rainbow Fish*. When asked what her favorite part was, she asserted that she didn't know yet, as she hadn't looked at the whole book. It was clear that Jasmine saw herself as a reader who could make informed decisions. She also regularly participated in our reading workshop shares. Jasmine soon discovered that there were books in the classroom that she could read all by herself. Ongoing conference records documented her engagement in this process. Asked to choose a just-right book at the end of the trimester for her reading portfolio, Jasmine identified a book with large illustrations accompanied by one line of text at the bottom. The text exactly matched the pictures, was set in a pattern, and contained some simple sight words.

Through her assessment folder, the picture of this emerging reader developed more completely. By the end of the first trimester, I knew that Jasmine knew all her upper-case letters, most of her lower-case letters, and most letter sounds. She had also started building up a sight-word vocabulary.

Jasmine showed continuous progress with her writing skills, keeping constant pace with the instruction offered. By the end of the first trimester, she could choose her topics with ease and made conscious decisions about the use of her writing time, choosing between writing personal narratives, messages, and signs. She always accompanied her beautifully detailed pictures with words that she had sourced from the environment, from books, or from sounding out. Her writing was fairly readable as she wrote her words with beginning and end sounds, sometimes incorporating middle sounds as well. Her stories continued to grow in detail, and she regularly shared them from the Author's Chair.

Middle of the Year

We begin to expand the reading workshop in the middle of the year. The essential question this trimester is: How do stories work?

LEARNING TARGETS FOR EXPANDING READING SKILLS	CONFERENCE QUESTIONS/ ANECDOTAL NOTES	ONGOING FORMATIVE ASSESSMENT
Readers retell stories.	What is happening in your story? Who is the story about? Where is the story happening? What is the problem? How is the problem getting solved?	Beginning, Middle, and End Parts of a Story 1 Parts of a Story 2 (all from Chapter 4)
Readers picture the story in their minds.	How do you think your character will act? What do you think this character might say? What do you think may happen in between these scenes? What kind of voice do you think the character will use?	
Readers predict what's going to happen next.	What do you think is going to happen next? What clues prompted you to make your prediction?	
Readers ask questions.	Do you have some questions about this story? Is this a discovery or a distracting question? What if . . . ? Does this story remind you of other stories?	

The main question for expanding the writing workshop in the middle of the year is: How do writers write stories?

LEARNING TARGETS FOR EXPANDING WRITING SKILLS	CONFERENCE QUESTIONS/ ANECDOTAL NOTES	ONGOING FORMATIVE ASSESSMENT
Exploring story planning.	Who is in your story? When is it taking place? Where is it taking place? What is the problem? How is the problem solved?	
Exploring story writing.		Student example of fiction: Evidence of • An understanding of beginning, middle, and end • Crafting a story title
Exploring story language.		Student example of fiction: Evidence of • Dialogues • Descriptions • Golden lines

Assessment in Action: A Look at Jasmine in the Middle of the Year

During the second trimester, Jasmine's anecdotal notes documented her enjoyment of playacting and performing fairy tales. She had assumed different roles—her favorite ones being that of a princess or a unicorn or a cat—and had made up stories and directed them with great energy. She also continued to expand her repertoire of reading skills. She was able to read independently for ten to fifteen minutes, choosing from both just-right books and books from the classroom library. She used many appropriate strategies to read, including using pictures and beginning sounds. Jasmine had excellent comprehension strategies and was able to retell main events in a story in sequence. She made personal connections with texts and had also started becoming aware of text-to-text connections. While reading *Mrs. Wishy-Washy's Tub*, for instance, Jasmine commented how the book reminded her of the other *Mrs. Wishy-Washy*, even though some of the animals were different. Toward the end of the trimester, I asked Jasmine to again identify a just-right book for her reading portfolio.

This time, the book she chose and read successfully had text on one side accompanied by an illustration on the other. There was an average of four lines of text per page, and the subject matched the picture. The reader would have to actually decode many of the words and be adept at "return sweep" (reading to the end of the line and then coming lower to start at the beginning of the next line) to successfully read this book.

By the second trimester Jasmine knew all the kindergarten-level sight words. With prompting, she was able to recall words from her environment and recognize them as she encountered them while reading. Jasmine's assessments showed that she was also very aware of sounds, rhymes, and syllables in words.

Jasmine embraced fiction writing with enthusiasm. Her published story showed evidence of story planning—characters, a setting, a problem, and a solution. It had a clear structure—a beginning, a middle, and an end—and beautiful language. The illustrations were meticulously planned and carried out. Jasmine took huge risks with her spelling, including beginning, middle, and end sounds. She consistently used spaces between words and mostly lower-case letters.

End of the Year

Toward the end of the year, I extend the reading and writing workshop by having the students independently apply the reading and writing strategies learned through the year. There is an emphasis on developing and sustaining self-extending systems.

The overarching essential question for reading is: How do readers pursue their interests? The students and I attempt to answer this question through exploring our reading personas, deepening our understanding and engagement with familiar genres and encountering newer ones. Mirroring the reading experience, the writing workshop is extended by exploring the question, How do writers express themselves through different genres? Even as they continue practicing writing in familiar genres, the students are exposed to and have the choice of choosing from newer ones.

Assessment in Action:
A Look at Jasmine at the End of the Year

Third-trimester conference and anecdotal records showed Jasmine's continued reading progress. She extended her reading to include newer genres such as nonfiction and poetry. She could identify and use text features within these genres. Her independent choice, however, was almost always fiction. Jasmine became increasingly confident in expressing her opinions about the books she read, comparing stories and authors with an ease born of her complete investment. At the end of the trimester, her choice of a just-right book was a book that accompanied many lines of text with an illustration that did not exactly match the subject of the text. The text did not follow any pattern and contained many sight words. The illustration on the other hand contained many clues that could lead the reader to interpret the story further. In conversations with Jasmine, I noticed that she was adept at using these pictures to imagine the story in her mind and to imagine scenes in between. She invested the characters with voices and expressions based on her interpretation of the story.

Jasmine had now progressed to a second set of sight words. She recognized and could write all her upper- and lower-case letters, and she also knew all the letter sounds. She could identify and write chunks within words and play around with word patterns.

Jasmine continued writing with engagement and enthusiasm and made conscious decisions about her writing every day. She wrote in a variety of genres, refining what she knew about writing personal narratives and fiction as well as exploring newer genres such as nonfiction and poetry. Her writing persona embraced several roles simultaneously—she was a storyteller, writing stories from her life; a story maker, creating tales of miracles and magic; a researcher, writing books on things she was an expert on; a poet, using words to evoke images; a letter writer, writing to communicate; and a sign maker, writing to define and designate.

It is clear that Jasmine had a very successful year in kindergarten. However, her case was by no means the average scenario in our classroom. There were some children who were not so receptive to instruction and a few who were marginally more so. The levels of skill, ability, and engagement through the year and through the different units of study were also very different. What was the same, however, was the system of record keeping that enabled me to differentiate and tailor my instruction according to individual needs. This system also recorded and celebrated the growth each student was making in different areas in a systematic manner.

EPILOGUE: ANNOUNCING AUDITIONS FOR NEW ROLES

Do you know Eric Carle and Leo Lionni write stories the same?" muses Brian. "Yeah, they both write about animals a lot. I think they like to write about animals," chimes in Roy. "And the animals always have problems," sighs Emma, subtly implying that the animals really should get on with their lives and not always be in one state of crisis or another. "But then it wouldn't be a story, right?" clarifies Josiah. "All stories need problems, and sometimes they are the same like in *The Mixed-Up Chameleon* and *A Color of His Own*." "That's just what I was saying," exclaims Brian, clearly delighted to have found classmates who can catch on to his thinking, clarify it, and even extend it. "I know chameleons change color," adds Daniel, pulling out an insect book from our nonfiction book basket and determinedly flipping pages to try to prove his point.

I overhear this ongoing animated discussion in a corner of our classroom where a small group of children have congregated in a book club to discuss authors they know and love. The group starts out with a few children but swells as more and more get pulled in from its fringes. I take notes and let the conversation wave its magic over me, ebbing and flowing with different ideas and diverse voices.

BRINGING IT ALL TOGETHER

During the last few weeks of the kindergarten year, I stress that readers and writers make choices about what they read and write. Sometimes, we wish to read or write for enjoyment and entertainment; sometimes we need to do so to seek or give information.

Reading workshop continues to unfold daily. The children have access to many different genres from our classroom library as well as the very large and popular collection of student-created work. I tell the children that skilled readers pursue their reading interests. Sometimes we do this independently; sometimes we do this with others who may be interested in the same things we are.

This is an ideal time to begin book clubs in the classroom. Book clubs add an extra dimension to our reading workshop. These clubs are simply small groups of children (four to six members) who choose to read the same book together or books similar in author, genre, or theme. The term *read* is of course based on its usage in kindergarten, as the members could also be listening as I read aloud to the group. The members then meet to talk about the book or books. I am a de facto member of each book club, and I rotate and participate as needed. Book clubs offer a fabulous opportunity for children to read books about subjects they are interested in along with like-minded peers. It gives everybody a chance to grow ideas through conversation. Since the groups are small, there is a greater chance of more voices being heard. The abilities are also mixed, and the students get a chance to work with a wider group, facilitating different interactions in the classroom.

The club meetings are scheduled during independent reading time. I introduce some possible club ideas to the whole class. A "favorite author" club, I tell the students, could read and discuss several books by the same author, such as Eric Carle, Leo Lionni, Kevin Henkes, Marcus Pfister, or Paulette Bourgeois. An "authors who write books with big messages" club could read books with similar messages by different authors—Eric Carle and Leo Lionni, for instance—and discuss how the big ideas in the book are similar though the story events may be different. A "favorite characters" club could read books about specific fictional characters like Franklin, Little Critter, or The Rainbow Fish, or even about fictional character types like princesses, dragons, or animals with magical powers. This club would discuss how the characters act, why they do so, and what their actions tell the reader about their thoughts and feelings. There could be clubs that read only a particular genre and talk about books in that genre; there could be clubs that read books with similar themes—families, school, or friends.

I write out some possibilities, and then we brainstorm other ideas as a group. After our list is complete, I narrow the offerings to a workable number. Too many possibilities would reduce the number of members in each group and make the clubs unworkable. I keep our original list to use for future club ideas. The children then sign up according to their interests.

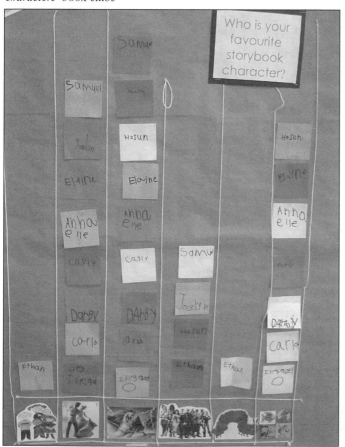

Sign-up for favorite characters' book clubs

We set up a schedule such that I can meet with each group over the course of the next two weeks. When we meet for the first time, I pass out copies of the book or books we are going to be reading, and I read aloud to the group over the next few meetings. We discuss our ideas, and I record the children's responses. After each meeting, we make plans for our next discussion. The books are available to the club members to browse through during their independent reading time, and I encourage the children to continue to explore them and bring their thoughts back to the next meeting.

Writing workshop offers similar opportunities for extension. By now, the children are familiar with writing in many genres, and I invite them to make conscious decisions about how they would like to fruitfully spend their workshop time. During writing workshop, Moria, Kayleigh, Meghan, Josiah, and Min Jae decide to write more fiction. Michelle has moved to a new house, Daniel has a new sister, and Arnav and Elijah need to record their stories about the recent earthquake that shook our town, so these children decide to write personal narratives. Jasmine wants to write her story about Helen Keller, based on the book that her second-grade sister read aloud to her. Brian and Cameron decide to make more information books, and Brian's will be about all the different animals he is fascinated with. Ellali has found that writing poetry is easy for her, as she needs to write short sentences and can churn out poem after poem.

My best hope for the children placed in my care for a year is that they will see themselves as readers and writers—that they will engage with reading and writing without any hesitation, negotiating text and print with the highest degree of engagement and investment. As I watch my class of kindergartners participate in daily reading and writing activities, I notice that they have their reading and writing personas firmly in place. These are not artificial personas but ones that they truly believe in, are proud of, and can uphold on their own terms. Moreover these personas are closely related, almost interdependent. They now embody the idea that I have modeled and reinforced at every opportunity, the idea that reading helps you become a better writer and that we write for others to read.

The last week of school Ellali cuddles up to me and hands me a much-scribbled sheet of paper. "This is for you," she says. I look at the paper, and it's a poem written by her, titled "Happy."

Happy
Mrs. Ranu
Makes me happy
Every day
On Tuesdays
That's all!

At a glance I notice several things about Ellali's writing. Ellali knows how to choose a genre that best suits her purpose and skill and knows she can create a powerful feeling with few words. She can write for a purpose and for an audience. Amazingly, in spite of the scribbles, the crossed-out lines, and the inventive spelling, I can read all the words. In the span of the past year, Ellali has made the connection between words, sounds, and their representative symbols. And she has made this leap happily and playfully, delighting in her new persona. That, indeed, is all.

All too soon it is time to say our final goodbyes. I stand silhouetted against the same doorway through which I welcomed the children. I watch my students skip down the kindergarten hallway, out into the brilliant summer sunshine. Under my breath I murmur, "And they lived happily ever after."

The End

APPENDIX

KINDERGARTEN LITERACY OVERVIEW

	Reading Workshop	Writing Workshop	Word-Study Activity Centers
TRIMESTER 1	Exploring the workshop: What are books? What are readers? Who reads? Where do we read? What do we read? How do readers get the message? Shared-reading focus / Read-aloud focus Comprehension focus / Student focus	Exploring the workshop: What is writing? Where do we find writing? Who writes? Why do writers write? How do we write? Focus lessons / Genre focus Celebration	Introducing early literacy concepts, letters, and sounds
TRIMESTER 2	Expanding the workshop: How do stories work? Shared-reading focus / Read-aloud focus Comprehension focus / Student focus	Expanding the workshop: How do writers write stories? Focus lessons / Genre focus Celebration	Manipulating letters and sounds
TRIMESTER 3	Extending the workshop: How do readers pursue their interests? Shared-reading focus / Read-aloud focus Comprehension focus / Student focus	Extending the workshop: How do writers express themselves through different genres? Focus lessons / Genre focus Celebration	Integrating and consolidating letter, sound, and word knowledge

BEGINNING, MIDDLE, AND END SHEET

Name of Story: _____

In the beginning . . .	In the middle . . .	In the end . . .

The Castle in the Classroom: Story as a Springboard for Early Literacy by Ranu Bhattacharyya. Copyright © 2010. Stenhouse Publishers.

PARTS OF A STORY 1 SHEET

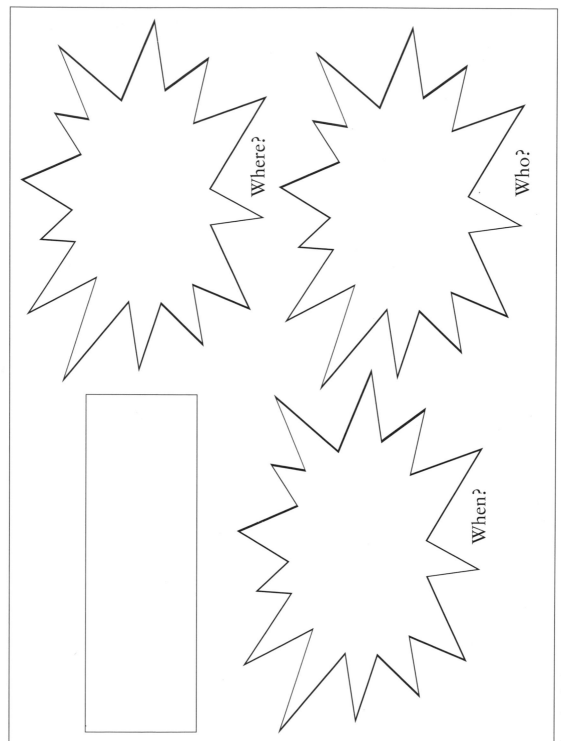

Where?

Who?

When?

The Castle in the Classroom: Story as a Springboard for Early Literacy by Ranu Bhattacharyya. Copyright © 2010. Stenhouse Publishers.

PARTS OF A STORY 2 SHEET

Problem?

_____

_____

Solved?

_____

_____

READING SURVEY

Do you like reading	Yes	No
Are you a good reader?	Yes	No
Do you have favorite books?	Yes	No
Do you like to talk about books?	Yes	No
Do you like to tell stories?	Yes	No

Where are you reading? _____

_____

_____

Who is reading with you? _____

_____

_____

What are you reading? _____

_____

_____

READING SURVEY (CONTINUED)

Draw a picture of you reading at home.

SELF-PORTRAIT FORM

Trimester 1	Trimester 2	Trimester 3
Name	Name	Name

The Castle in the Classroom: Story as a Springboard for Early Literacy by Ranu Bhattacharyya. Copyright © 2010. Stenhouse Publishers.

CONFERENCE RECORD FORM

Conference Notes: _____

The Castle in the Classroom: Story as a Springboard for Early Literacy by Ranu Bhattacharyya. Copyright © 2010. Stenhouse Publishers.

READING CONFERENCE QUESTIONS

First Trimester	Second Trimester
Why did you choose this book?	What is happening in your story? Who is the story about? Where is the story happening? What is the problem? How is the problem getting solved?
Do you like/not like the story? Why? Do you have a favorite part?	How do you think your character will act? What do you think this character might say? What do you think may happen in between these scenes? What kind of voice do you think the character will use?
Does this remind you of something • In your life? • In another book? • In the world around you?	What do you think is going to happen next? What clues prompted you to make your prediction?
How did you choose this book? Did you • Look at the cover? • Look at the title? • Look at the pictures? • Look at the words? • Choose a book you've heard before?	Do you have some questions about this story? Is this a discovery or a distracting question? What if . . . ? Does this story remind you of other stories?
How are you reading this book? Are you • Starting from the first page? • Turning the pages one by one? • Using a library voice? • Using the library correctly? • Practicing partner reading?	
What strategy are you using to read? Are you • Looking at the pictures? • Looking at the words? • Stretching words out like a rubber band and sounding them out? Can you show me how you are reading?	
Are there some words you can recognize?	

The Castle in the Classroom: Story as a Springboard for Early Literacy by Ranu Bhattacharyya. Copyright © 2010. Stenhouse Publishers.

WRITING CONFERENCE QUESTIONS

First Trimester	Second Trimester
What is your drawing about? Can you show me some details you've added to make your drawing look real?	Who is in your story? When is it taking place? Where is it taking place? What is the problem? How is the problem solved?
What are you writing about? How did you know what to write?	
What is your story about? What is happening in your story?	
What strategy are you using to write the words to your story? Are you • Sounding words out? • Writing quick-and-easy words? • Writing words you recognize? • Writing words from dictionaries? • Writing words the best you can? Can you reread your writing?	
Can you tell me the story over your fingers? Have you written the outside and inside of your story?	

The Castle in the Classroom: Story as a Springboard for Early Literacy by Ranu Bhattacharyya. Copyright © 2010. Stenhouse Publishers.

BIBLIOGRAPHY

CHILDREN'S BOOKS

While the titles listed here are books that I found useful to teach particular focus lessons, there are surely many other great books that I have not used or listed. Moreover, many of these books are at a much higher decoding level than expected of a kindergartner. This is especially true of the fairy tales. I wanted my students to be able to dive into books with confidence and not be limited by their decoding skills. If I had to identify a hallmark for the books I chose, it would be that they all have vibrant pictures that my students could use to retell the stories. This list is therefore a suggested resource; it is not restrictive or exhaustive in any form.

Amery, Heather. *The Story of Rumpelstiltskin.*
Appleby, Ellen. *The Three Billy Goats Gruff.*
Bourgeois, Paulette. Franklin series.
Bridwell, Norman. Clifford series.
Carle, Eric. *The Very Hungry Caterpillar.*
    The Mixed-Up Chameleon.
    The Grouchy Ladybug.
    The Very Lonely Firefly.
    The Very Busy Spider.
    The Very Clumsy Click Beetle.
    The Very Quiet Cricket.
    Today Is Monday.
    Dream Snow.
    Pancakes, Pancakes!
    The Art of Eric Carle.

Child, Lauren. *Beware of the Storybook Wolves.*
Cowley, Joy. Mrs. Wishy-Washy series.
  The Meanie series.
  Huggles series.
Craft, K. Y. *Cinderella.*
  Sleeping Beauty.
Daniel, Alan. *The More We Get Together.*
Dematons, Charlotte. *The Yellow Balloon.*
Disney, R. H. *Snow White and the Seven Dwarves.*
  Cinderella.
Edgar, Amy. *The Little Mermaid.*
Gliori, Debi. *No Matter What.*
Granowsky, Alvin. *Help Yourself, Little Red Hen.*
Henkes, Kevin. The Mouse books.
Joosse, Barbara M. *Mama, Do You Love Me?*
Lillie, Patricia. *When This Box Is Full.*
Lionni, Leo. *A Color of His Own.*
Little, Jean, Maggie De Vries, and Phoebe Gilman. *Once Upon a Golden Apple.*
Mayer, Marianna. *Beauty and the Beast.*
  The Adventures of Tom Thumb.
Mayer, Mercer. Little Critter series.
McCafferty, Catherine. *Rapunzel.*
  The Gingerbread Man.
McGhee, Alison. *Countdown to Kindergarten.*
McQueen, Lucinda. *The Little Red Hen.*
Ottolenghi, Carol. *Jack and the Beanstalk.*
Parkes, Brenda, and Judith Smith. *The Enormous Watermelon.*
Pfister, Marcus. Rainbow Fish series.
Pocock, Rita. *The Land of Many Colors.*
Ransom, Candice. *Goldilocks and the Three Bears.*
  Little Red Riding Hood.
Rose, Deborah Lee, and Carey Armstrong-Ellis. *The Twelve Days of Kindergarten.*
Shannon, David. The David books.
Siebert, Patricia. *The Three Little Pigs.*
Slate, Joseph. Miss Bindergarten series.
Tafuri, Nancy. *Will You Be My Friend? A Bunny and Bird Story.*
Teitelbaum, Michael. *Sleeping Beauty.*
Trivizas, Eugene. *The Three Little Wolves and the Big Bad Pig.*

Wick, Walter. *Can You See What I See? Once Upon a Time.*
Young, Ed. *Lon Po Po: A Red-Riding Hood Story from China.*
Zelinsky, Paul. *Rapunzel.*
   Rumpelstiltskin.

PROFESSIONAL LITERATURE

Boushey, Gail, and Joan Moser. 2006. *The Daily Five.* Portland, ME: Stenhouse.

Brown, Judy Sorum. 2006. "Fire." In *A Leader's Guide to Reflective Practice.* Bloomington, IN: Trafford.

Calkins, Lucy McCormick. 2000. *The Art of Teaching Reading.* Allyn and Bacon.

Calkins, Lucy, et al. 2003. *Units of Study for Primary Writing: A Yearlong Curriculum.* Portsmouth, NH: Heinemann.

Campbell Hill, Bonnie, 2001. *Developmental Continuums.* Norwood, MA: Christopher Gordon.

Campbell Hill, Bonnie, Cynthia Ruptic, and Lisa Norwick. 1998. *Classroom Based Assessment.* Norwood, MA: Christopher Gordon.

Clay, Marie. 1991. *Becoming Literate: The Construction of Inner Control.* Portsmouth, NH: Heinemann.

———. 2000. *Concepts About Print: What Have Children Learned About the Way We Print Language?* Portsmouth, NH: Heinemann.

———. 2006. *An Observation Survey of Early Literacy Achievement.* Portsmouth, NH: Heinemann.

———. 2007a. *Reading Recovery: Stones.* Portsmouth, NH: Heinemann.

———. 2007b. *Reading Recovery: Sand.* Portsmouth, NH: Heinemann.

Collins, Kathy. 2004. *Growing Readers.* Portland, ME: Stenhouse.

Cunningham, Andie, and Ruth Shagoury. 2005. *Starting with Comprehension.* Portland, ME: Stenhouse.

Diller, Debbie. 2003. *Literacy Work Stations.* Portland, ME: Stenhouse.

Duthie, Christine. 1996. *True Stories: Nonfiction Literacy in the Primary Classroom.* Portland, ME: Stenhouse.

Fisher, Bobbi. 1998. *Joyful Learning in Kindergarten.* Portsmouth, NH: Heinemann.

Fletcher, Ralph. 2007. *How to Write Your Life Story.* New York: HarperCollins.

Fletcher, Ralph, and JoAnn Portalupi. 1998. *Craft Lessons: Teaching Writing K–8.* Portland, ME: Stenhouse.

———. 2007. *Craft Lessons: Teaching Writing K–8.* 2nd ed. Portland, ME: Stenhouse.

Fountas, Irene, and Gay Su Pinnell. 2001. *Guided Reading: Good First Teaching for All Children.* Portsmouth, NH: Heinemann.

———. 2006. *Teaching for Comprehending and Fluency.* Portsmouth, NH: Heinemann.

Fox, Mem. 2008. *Reading Magic: Why Reading Aloud to Our Children Will Change Their Lives Forever.* New York: Mariner.

Franzese, Rosalie. 2002. *Reading and Writing in Kindergarten.* New York: Scholastic.

Gentry, J. Richard. 2006. *Breaking the Code.* Portsmouth, NH: Heinemann.

Harvey, Stephanie, and Anne Goudvis. 2000. *Strategies That Work: Teaching Comprehension to Enhance Understanding.* Portland, ME: Stenhouse.

Harwayne, Shelley. 2000. *Lifetime Guarantees.* Portsmouth, NH: Heinemann.

Heard, Georgia. 1999. *Awakening the Heart.* Portsmouth, NH: Heinemann.

Horn, Martha, and Mary Ellen Giacobbe. 2007. *Talking, Drawing, Writing: Lessons for Our Youngest Writers.* Portland, ME: Stenhouse.

Johnson, Pat. 2006. *One Child at a Time.* Portland, ME: Stenhouse.

Keene, Ellin Oliver, and Susan Zimmermann. 1997. *Mosaic of Thought: Teaching Comprehension in a Reader's Workshop.* Portsmouth, NH: Heinemann.

Miller, Debbie. 2002. *Reading with Meaning: Teaching Comprehension in the Primary Grades.* Portland, ME: Stenhouse.

Pinell, Gay Su, and Irene C. Fountas. 1998. *Word Matters.* Portsmouth, NH: Heinemann.

———. 2003. *Phonics Lessons.* Portsmouth, NH: Heinemann.

Ray, Katie Wood, with Lisa Cleaveland. 2004. *About the Authors.* Portsmouth, NH: Heinemann.

Reid, Janine, and Betty Shultze. 2005. *What's Next for This Beginning Writer?* Portland, ME: Stenhouse.

Routman, Regie. 1994. *Invitations: Changing as Teachers and Learners K–12.* Portsmouth, NH: Heinemann.

———. 2000. *Teaching Kindergarteners How to Love Writing Poetry.* New York: Scholastic.

———. 2002. *Reading Essentials.* Portsmouth, NH: Heinemann.

———. 2004. *Writing Essentials*. Portsmouth, NH: Heinemann.

Taberski, Sharon. 2000. *On Solid Ground*. Portsmouth, NH: Heinemann.

Wells, Gordon. 1985. *The Meaning Makers: Children Learning Language and Using Language to Learn*. Portsmouth, NH: Heinemann.